THROWN TO THE WOLVES

Thrown To The Wolves

ARABELLA WINTERS

ISBN 10: 1-59298-301-4
ISBN 13: 978-1-59298-301-8

Library of Congress Control Number: 2009933534
Printed in the United States of America
First Printing: 2010
14   13   12   11   10   5   4   3   2   1

Cover design by Fritz Rud
Interior design by Ryan Scheife, Mayfly Design

Any persons within the cover photograph are models and the images are used for illustrative purposes only.

BEAVER'S POND
PRESS

Beaver's Pond Press, Inc.
7104 Ohms Lane, Suite 101
Edina, MN 55439-2129
(952) 829-8818
www.BeaversPondPress.com

To order, visit www.BeaversPondBooks.com
or call (800) 901-3480. Reseller discounts available.

WITH LOVE . . .

Anne

You have changed my understanding of the world in too many ways to mention here. Through your modeling (and much needed encouragement) I have learned how to both listen to and follow my heart. With your unconditional love and guidance, you've held my hand as I've moved through my pain into freedom and light. You truly are a mother to me. I love you.

Laurie

Thank you, Laurie, for breathing love into my battered little heart at a time when death seemed to be such a better option. You're my advocate, my mirror, my partner in crime (think Lake Powell), and you bring new meaning to the phrase, "Remember when?" You're the sister I never had and my best friend. Never forget our future date with the Italian CNAs—my calendar is marked!

PEBBLEPATH

A stony path
One that I have crossed
Alone on a black
Moonlit trail
As I approach
Hard and cold
I find my heart beating
What will I be?
When do I get there?
Will I know who I see?
Light and silky
Black night calling me
Silently walking
Moon halfway
Lighting the pathway
Hollowing like a tree trunk
Closer as I go

—Krista Boggess

FORWARD

By Anne Katherine

Author of *Boundaries, Where to Draw the Line, Anatomy of a Food Addiction, When Misery Is Company, When Someone You Love Eats Too Much,* and *How to Make Almost Any Diet Work.*

A little girl cowers in a closet. A young teen gets beaten for waiting ten minutes to feed the dog. A young woman tries to take her life—and her mother reacts with irritation at the inconvenience.

Raw, real, honest—here is the true story of a woman's crossing from chaos into a generous and purposeful life. If you, too, have survived a childhood of danger or sexual predation, then you'll find here a sister in courage and a guide to self-deliverance.

We can know on an intellectual level that childhood abuse causes harm. But if we've been lucky enough to escape it, we may not comprehend how abuse soaks through the pores into the very cells of a child. We may not realize that being steeped in abuse pollutes possibilities, choices, and perspective.

This memoir is more than a window into the life of a tortured child. It is a rare opportunity to actually experience the hope and despair, the suspense and the awakening, of a child viewed not for herself, but for her use to the adults in her family.

A secret also gets ripped open—the horrifying secret that, sometimes, a mother will sacrifice a child on the altar of her own needs.

We're not talking here of the normal structuring a parent has to do to get herself fed or rested, or the compromises we all make in order to keep the family's economy afloat. No, this is something entirely different.

We tend to think of abused mothers as innocent victims held in thrall to their abusers, and that often is the truth. But another reality also exists, and it's hard to gulp down. Sometimes, a parent will toss her child into the abuser's arms to keep those arms and that terrifying attention away from herself. She may even be willing to forfeit her child's well-being (and self-esteem and future peace of mind) to get something she wants.

Allow yourself to open to the gritty passion of a woman who dares to unlock *all* the secrets.

Prepare to care.

MY NOTE TO YOU, MY READER

I am using pseudonyms for all people, animals, and locations in this book to protect their identities to the best of my ability. My goal is to shed light on child abuse and the devastation and confusion that it caused in my life. I do not wish to bring shame or harm to any of the people mentioned in this book. I believe that they have suffered enough in their own pain and I wish peace and love for each and every one of them.

This book is a collection of some of my memories. I have put forth every effort to be precise with the specific ages during which all events occurred. When uncertain of exact age, I used the street name (fictitious) of the home in which I was residing at the time, as well as my probable age range.

I am aware that memory can be imperfect, therefore I say that this book is "based on a true story." Having said that, I want you, the reader, to know that I've recounted my experience with the utmost accuracy and integrity.

This is my account. This is my experience.

This is my story.

ACKNOWLEDGMENTS

Sweet Don . . . Thank you for your continuous belief in me, especially during those periods when I was having a difficult time believing in myself. Throughout our thirteen-year-long friendship, you have consistently offered your support and rescued me from many a sticky situation. Your generosity has opened a world of opportunities that I didn't believe were possible for a gal like me. Thank you, Don, for supporting me in living my dream. I can't imagine my life without you.

What a blessing to have you in my life, Krista! I cherish our bond and will always look forward to our supportive early morning chats—my Krista fixes. Thank you for your friendship, love, understanding, trust, and outstanding editing abilities. I'll forever remember the two elderly ladies and the elderly man (stuffed in the back seat) whom we pulled up next to at a stoplight. I'll continue to laugh hysterically when I think of the look on Rube's face (stuffed into *our* back seat) when he looked over; the knowing glance that he and the old man shared is forever etched in my mind.

Rube, Rube, Rube. You have been an angel in my life. You had my back and kept me safe from harm when I was self-destructing with drugs and alcohol. When all I saw and felt was darkness, you comforted me by rubbing my feet and brushing my hair for hours on end. You invited me into your family on those days of the year during which family is stressed, you made me laugh so hard that I could feel the joy in every cell of my being, and you taught me that there are men in the world whom I can love and trust. Thank you for being my rock, my teacher, my pocket homie, and a great love in my life.

This acknowledgement would not be complete without thanking all of the wonderful people who have entered my life to teach me about myself. Whether these walking wise men and women are aware of it or not, each and every one of them—professors, classmates, friends, acquaintances, those I met by chance in random encounters who shared the gifts of their wisdom, intentionally or otherwise—has changed my life. To each and every person who has entered my life, I thank you for your gifts.

And last but not least, I must thank my guides, teachers, angels, Source energy, and nature for grounding me, reminding me of my goodness, and totally loving me. I would not be who I am without these profound connections.

TWENTY-NINE YEARS OLD

(Day One, 4:02 p.m.)

I don't understand how this happened. How did I end up here? Have the past six years meant nothing? What good does therapy do if I can still end up in this painful and familiar place? I've done so much work on myself. I've overcome so much. Could it be that this was all a mistake? Or was this just another lesson I needed to learn before I could truly be ready for the real thing?

I needed some matches, so I went looking in some drawers and eventually in his bedroom. I don't know what came over me. It was as if some crazed woman took over my body for those few minutes. As I started rummaging through his drawers and boxes, under his bed and in his clothes hamper, I looked up and into the mirror and saw my long brown hair and my pale skin, but the white eyes of a wild woman. I knew I was going to find something.

Our relationship had become increasingly strained over the past six months, so strained that I knew that something wasn't right. I just didn't know what it was yet. But much to my horror, I was about to find out.

I found a box labeled "Misc. Tools." I was a ravenous animal. I ripped it open, knowing that I would find something incriminating inside. And I did.

SMACK!

I looked at the clock. It was a few minutes before all of my friends were to show up and my world had just come crashing down on me. I wanted to cancel. I needed to cancel. I can't do this. I can't feel this. I can't feel this. I CAN'T FEEL THIS! I wanted to curl up into a little ball on the floor and fall asleep. I wanted all of this to be a dream. This has to be a dream. This has to be a dream. This has to be a dream!

That's when I began lying. To myself. I had to come up with some way to believe that this wasn't the truth. This could be someone else's. Maybe he's holding *it* for his roommate, Jon. Maybe his friend Patrick needed him to hold *it* because his wife wouldn't approve. Maybe *it's* from a long, long time ago. That's why *it's* in a box. He's just moved all of his boxes from his last house, so maybe *it's* been in one of those boxes for years. Maybe. Maybe. Maybe.

As much as I tried to imagine all the ways that this couldn't be happening, reality was slipping under the crack of denial's door and shooting straight through my heart. I suddenly realized the absurdity of what I was telling myself.

He has no reason to hold *it* for his roommate, none at all. His roommate had no one coming to visit that would object to him having *it*. And if he were holding *it* for Patrick, then he wouldn't have needed to hide *it* in our house. He could have just stuck *it* in his drawer, or some other obvious place in the house. It was clear *it* was being hidden from me.

Even though I wasn't technically living in the house, I was planning on moving the bulk of my belongings in after I graduated from college. But I came over to the house all the time to paint, especially during the day when he was at work.

The biggest blow to my denial was the stereo faceplate container. A blinding fragment of reality was inside this container. That's where I found *it*. As I picked up the Alpine container, I began running through my memory. I was trying to remember when we bought the Alpine. Did he have this stereo before I loaned him money to buy his truck? This could be the stereo from his last car.

That's when I felt like someone had punched me in the stomach. Suddenly I couldn't breathe. My head felt as if it was about to float right off of my body. Confusion swirled around me. Nothing made sense. This couldn't be happening.

We bought this stereo during our first Christmas together. I got him a gift certificate to Stereo Palace and he bought the Alpine with that gift certificate.

SMACK!

Reality hit me.

SMACK! SMACK-SMACK!!

OH FUCK! He's been lying to me. This can't be happening. This can't be fucking happening.

FIVE TO SIX YEARS OLD

I'm in a little yellow trailer in Otis, Kansas. I think I am five or six years old. I could be younger; it's hard to tell. It's dark outside. I'm sleeping on the floor with my three cousins and my older brother. We are under blankets in the living room. It's my aunt and uncle's trailer.

This is where my mom sends me every summer: Otis, Kansas. It feels like we're here all summer. It feels like a really long time to be away from home. I like it, but I don't. When I'm here I'm not as afraid as I am when I'm at my house in Montana. The only person that I have to be afraid of here is my brother. But he doesn't hit me as much when I'm here. He's still mean to me, but not as mean as he usually is.

We come to Otis to stay at my grandma's house, but we visit my aunt and uncle and cousins because they live right down the road. My grandma doesn't like me. She only likes boys. My grandpa is nice to me and the other girls. My brother is always mean to me. But my boy cousin likes me a lot. He makes me feel special.

I wake up and feel him between my legs. He is licking me down there. It feels really good. It feels bad. He tells me to be quiet and not to tell anyone. His lips are chapped and crackly. I don't like it. It feels gross and icky. What if my other cousins wake up? What if my brother sees?

It feels good. It feels good. Between my legs feels good.

When he's done, he tells me again not to tell anyone. He tells me that it's okay for him to do that since we aren't blood-related. I don't know what that means. But he also tells me that I can't tell anyone.

So I don't.

Not for a gazillion years.

TWENTY-TWO YEARS OLD

My head is pounding. Throbbing. Aching. I feel hot. I'm so hot. Hot. Hot. Hot. I think I was hit by a truck. I feel like I've been run over. I'm so thirsty. I could drink a gallon of water right now. I need water. I need water. I need water. Not again. Not again.

What did I do last night? I can't remember. When I open my eyes, what am I going to see? Will what I see jog a memory of last night's escapade? Will I again be stabbed by the shame that overcomes every nerve in my body when I realize I've slept with another guy that I don't know?

As I roll over and slowly force my swollen, thirsty eyelids open, I see a huge body in my bed next to me. OH, SHIT! What the fuck happened last night? Who is this person and how did he get in my bed?

I lie here and think. Think. Think. Think harder. What happened?

FLASH!
Being on stage.

FLASH!
Blue and red cop lights flashing into the car as I am in and out of consciousness. In the back seat of Kallie's car.

FLASH!
A simulated orgasm.

FLASH!
Two big black men getting into the car.

FLASH!
Bachelorette #3!!

FLASH!
Kissing one of the black guys.

FLASH! FLASH!
Won a date with a really handsome bachelor.

FLASH!
The dating game at a bar . . .

More memories flood my mind. I was at a bar with my roommate
and friend, Kallie. A local radio station and one of its most
popular DJs was holding a contest. The Dating Game contest.
Three single girls chosen from the audience to vie for the
attentions of a handsome bachelor. Answer questions. He chooses
the lucky winner based on what answers he likes. The audience
applause helps him decide.

I don't know how I got up on stage. I vaguely remember
being on stage. I remember seeing the hot bachelor blindfolded
at the end of the stage. I remember there being two other girls on
stage with me. Lots of cheering and hollering from the audience. I
have no clear memory of what the other girls looked like. I know
that they were both pretty, though. I was nervous. I thought,
They are better than me.

I remember a sea of endless faces staring at me from the
audience. I remember answering questions, but I don't know what
they were—except for one: Can you act as if you are having an
orgasm?

FLASH!
"Oh . . . ahhhh . . . umm . . . ummmmm . . . oh, yeah, uhhh
. . . uhhh . . . uhhh . . . oh, yeah." I go on and on. The audience is
going wild. I feel no shame. My goal is to be sexy, sultry, to have
every man in the audience want me. To have every woman in the
audience wish that she were me. I have to win, I NEED TO BE THE
SEXIEST! I AM THE SEXIEST!! Every man in the audience wants
me. I NEED TO BE THE SEXIEST!

Cheering for bachelorette #1: Loud. She's better than me.

Cheering for bachelorette #2: Louder. She's definitely better than me.

Cheering for bachelorette #3: Raise the roof! How could she be better than me?

And the winner is: bachelorette #3!!! I WON! I AM THE SEXIEST! I NEED THIS! I GOT THIS. I AM A WINNER! I feel so good. Full. Valuable. Alive. WANTED. WANTED. WANTED. WANTED.

I win a T-shirt and a date with the bachelor. I talk to the bachelor. He gives me his number. He is way too stupid for me. Maybe he's just nervous. I don't care. I walk away in search of a real man to spend the night with. He's not the one for tonight . . .

As I scan my memory for any indication of how the man in my bed appeared here, I come up with nothing. I have no idea what his name is, where I met him, if we fucked. How am I going to sneak out of the room without him seeing me?

I just do.

I creep downstairs to see if Kallie is awake. There is another man on the floor, sleeping. I walk past him and go into Kallie's room. I ask her, "What happened last night?"

She tells me. We went to The Drinking Hole. I was in a Dating Game Contest. I didn't like the bachelor. We got hit on by a couple of black guys. They came home with us. On the way home, we got pulled over. Kallie got a DWI.

I slipped in and out of consciousness the whole way home. We got home and I woke up. I went into the bedroom with the biggest black guy. That's where the story ends for Kallie. She doesn't know what happened for me in the bedroom. She knows I was totally shit-faced. She knows I won the contest. She knows she's fucked because of the DWI. She is fucked. Fucked. Fucked.

Fucked. She doesn't have it in her to care about whether or not I am fucked. She's really fucked.

As we talk, I look down and see that the zipper on my pants is broken open. Like someone was trying to get my pants off and ripped the zipper open in the process. There is dried white stuff all along the zipper. There is dried cum along the zipper. There is fucking dried cum along the zipper! Fucking dried cum!!

I don't know if we fucked. I don't want to ask. I don't even want to go back upstairs and see the men. I just want it to be night so I can drink all of this away. I have to drink all of this away. I can't think about this.

FLASH!
Big black man on top of me.

FLASH!
A simulated orgasm . . .

I must get high. I can't think about this anymore. Erase last night. I must erase last night. I have to erase last night. No more. Drink. I have to get high.

Shame, shame, fucking shame. I have to quit drinking. But I *need* to drink right now. I can't do this anymore. I have to stop. I am disgusting. I am a whore. None of my friends do this; what is wrong with me?!?!? I am so disgusting. I am a loser. I don't deserve good. I am bad. I am bad. I have to quit drinking or I will die. I have to quit drugs or I will die. I can't live like this. God, I need a drug right now.

I smoke a bowl and start to drink.

My mom is right. I am a slut.

SEVENTEEN YEARS OLD

I have the plastic bag in my lap. Actually, it's two bags. Inside each bag there are 120 sleeping pills. One dose for each of us. We need that much because the last time we tried to end it we didn't take enough and we only ended up being sick for the three days that followed.

But this time there is no we. We are not going to do anything. I can't wait that long. I have to end this now. And I'm guaranteed to end it if I take the pills from both bags. That would make at least 240 sleeping pills. That would do it. End it. End it. No more pain.

This will all be over. Over. Over. Fucking Over.

I look at the bag and decide that it's now or never. I walk to my bedroom door. Shit. I'm going to have to pass my mom's boyfriend on the way out there. What if he notices that I'm taking the whole jug of juice into my room?

Fuck it. Just go.

I reach for the door handle. Open it. I go straight down the hallway and to the fridge and take out the orange juice container. As I close the fridge door, I look over at my mom's boyfriend sitting on the couch watching TV. He doesn't look up. He's so angry at me. I can't believe he called me a fuck-up. He hates me. They all hate me. They all fucking hate me. *I* fucking hate me. I'll be better off dead. They'll be better off if I'm dead. My heart sinks. Breaks. It's heavy and hurts like I've never felt it hurt.

He's never even raised his voice at me, let alone tell me that I'm a big fuck-up. That I'm ruining the lives of everyone around me. He's right. I am a big fuck-up. I don't even deserve to be walking the earth. All I do is hurt people. All I do is cause people pain. None of my friends are this fucked up. I'm bad. There is something seriously wrong with me.

I start to walk back to my room. I go in and close the door. Lock it. I sit on my mattress. I decided a while ago that I wanted my mattress on the ground. I didn't want a bed frame anymore. I needed to know that nothing could get under my bed and grab me in the night. I always feared someone grabbing me in the night. While I'm sleeping.

I sit on my bed. I stare at the two bags of white pills. There are a ton of them. I think for a couple of minutes. Can I do this? Can I really do this?

I scan my memory for anything at all over the recent past that will allow me to see it differently . . . nothing.

FLASH!

I see the cops coming to my school and questioning me about the police jackets that I stole from their precious little cop cars. I see me snitching on my friends. I see me telling the pigs that I gave the jackets away. I did. I gave all three of them to three different people. I see those people very angry at me. They definitely hate me. Especially Gavin.

Gavin's parents were drug dealers. Nothing serious that I know about, just pot. But even pot dealers don't like it when the po-po show up on their doorstep looking for their precious little cop jackets . . .

Oink. Oink. Fucking Oink. I hate the fucking pigs. If it weren't for them, none of this would be happening. I wouldn't have to take these fucking pills.

Three felonies. One for each jacket. FUCK! FUCK! FUCK!

Then I see more.

FLASH!

I see myself at the Sears in Helena, Montana. That was a short while after the cops showed up at school. I see me and my friend Ellie going into the dressing room and stuffing dresses into our purses. We did it all the time. In fact, we had been doing it for years. We'd done it regularly since I was in the seventh grade.

Go to a store wearing big skirts and sweaters, or carrying a big purse. Put on clothes that we find at the store under our own clothes. Or stuff them in our purses, whatever works. Take what we want. These huge corporations have too much money anyway. It's not as if we're stealing from people we know. I would never do that. That's wrong.

We walk out of the store. We look at each other. There's someone following us. Should we run? What the fuck should we do? Should we run? We search each other's eyes for a sign that would point us in the right direction.

Too late.

"Excuse me, ladies. You need to come with us."

The man takes us to a back room where the security guard wants to strip search us. We tell him he's a fucking loser. We say it to him a thousand times. FUCKING LOSER! . . .

There's another felony. Felony shoplifting. FUCK! FUCK! FUCK! FUCK! I'm fucked!

Now I see earlier today.

FLASH!

We get home from Helena and sneak out of our houses to meet up. We hitchhike to see each other. We have a plan. We're going to her grandma and grandpa's. They're in Florida or some warm place where they spend the winters like most old people who have lots of money and want to get away from the cold weather do.

We're stealing their car and taking off to California. Ellie's been there before. We'll figure out the rest of the plan once we get there.

We arrive at Ellie's grandparents' house. How the fuck are we sup-posed to get inside? How do we get into the car? We have no keys. We'll break a window. Yeah, we'll break a window.

They're all triple-pane. So we case the joint. We find a window that is the most inconspicuous and at ground level. We find a huge rock. We take turns throwing it.

SMASH!

We break the first pane. SHIT. IT'S SO LOUD! We need to do this quickly.

My blood is pumping. I'm higher than I've been in a really long time. And I'm pretty much high all day, every day. Have been since I was thirteen years old. This is different. I can feel the blood rushing through my veins. I can feel my heart pounding. My ribs vibrate from the pounding. I'm so fucking high.

I look at Ellie. I can tell she's as high as me. I can see her heart pounding through her chest. She looks at me. We have to hurry it up.

SMASH!

The second pane breaks. Glass flies everywhere. It's not a clean break. The window is huge. This is going to take some work. She looks at me again.

SMASH!

Last one. We're in. We just have to creep through the shards and we're in.

We get inside. We start scanning the house. What can we take? We have no money. Fuck. Fuck. Fuck. No money! FUCK!

Jackpot! The hugest, fullest liquor cabinet ever. Now all we need are the keys to the car. We find the keys to the Saab and we load the car full of booze. We steal some Mexican money from their bedroom. Coins and bills. We don't care that it's Mexican. All that matters is that it's money.

We get into the car. What the fuck? The gears aren't fucking labeled!

We turn on the car, but we can't figure out how to get it into reverse. How are we supposed to get it out of the fucking garage? We're getting frustrated. Having second thoughts. Maybe we shouldn't do this. Maybe we should just go home and face the music.

No, we have to go. We have to run away. There's nothing for us here. I'm hated. Everyone hates me. I'm a thief, a drug addict, a snitch, a felon, a fucking liar. Everyone hates me. I need a new life.

DING-DONG.

OH SHIT! Someone's at the door. We look. It's the cops. The fucking cops again. I've seen enough of them to last me a lifetime. What are we going to say? We need a story. What are we going to fucking say?

Too late . . .

Felony number five. Attempted burglary. Or breaking and entering, or some other fucking felonious charge. FUCK! FUCK! FUCK! FUCK! FUCK!

I stare at the pills for one last second before I decide that the last two felonies have pushed me over the edge. I can't live like this. I'm a loser. I'm always going to be unhappy. I hate myself. Everyone else hates me. I'm a fucking no-good loser and I need to die.

I shove fistful after fistful of pills into my mouth. The orange juice isn't enough to wipe out the shake-my-head-in-disgust bitterness at the back of my throat and all along my tongue. I finish the first bag and move on to the next.

Handful after handful of bitter nastiness. I can hardly stand it. I take bigger and bigger swigs of juice with every handful. All I taste is Pill. Pill. Pill. Nasty fucking Pill.

I look down.

It's done. They're all gone. I took them all. I get out my notebook and write a goodbye letter. Something like I can't take it anymore. I can't do this. Blah, blah, fucking blah.

I lie in bed for a while and start to feel dizzy. This is really it. I took enough to definitely kill me. Definitely. No questions asked. I'm going to die.

I call Ellie. I tell her I couldn't wait. I took our stockpile. She gets mad. She yells, "YOU TOOK MINE?"

She snaps, *"You didn't wait for me?!?!?"*

I couldn't wait, I told her.

She snarls, "Fine, I guess I'll see you in hell."

We hang up. I'm ready to die. I'm fading off.

I'm getting drowsy . . .

SEVEN TO NINE YEARS OLD
House on Pine Road

From the shower my mom yells.

"CLEAN UP YOUR ROOM. IT'S A PIGSTY!"

I look at my best friend, Karen, and smile. In my most mocking voice I say, "Clean up your room; it's a pigsty." I smile at my friend.

Big mistake. Big, big mistake. I hear my mom say to my step-dad, Bill, "Take care of her!"

Loud stomping across the floor of the house. The stomping is coming this way. Oh no! He's mad and he's coming in here. I look over at Karen and she sees my fear and suddenly she looks afraid too.

Bill has been around for a while now. They force me to call him Dad now that they are married. I have to call him Dad and if I don't, I get spanked. I try to remember, but I'm not used to calling anyone Dad. He is so scary. He is really, really big. He's almost as tall as my bedroom door. And I am always in a lot of trouble when he's around. I don't like him at all. I wish my mom never met him.

The only good thing about Bill is his kitty, Rusty. I love Rusty. I love having something soft and fluffy to pet and love. The only thing about Rusty is that he loves to number one and number two on my shoes. I hate that. But I love him because he doesn't hurt me. Just my shoes.

Sometimes I find poo in the back of my closet that is all white, like marshmallows. I'd eat 'em if they were marshmallows. But I can't because they're old Rusty number twos.

I turn around and see Bill standing at my doorway. He asks me what I just said. I quietly shrink. I tell him I didn't say anything. He asks me again, "WHAT DID YOU SAY?"

I tell him, "Nothing."

I shrink more. I'm as tiny as my Barbies and he's as big as a building.

SMACK!

I go flying across the room. I hit the bed and start crying. There is blood everywhere. I hear someone else crying. I look over and my best friend is bawling. She says over and over I want to go home. I forgot she was here. She wants to go home and she's crying.

My nose hurts. There is blood everywhere. Blood everywhere. Red blood is everywhere. It's on the bed, on my face, on the sheets, on my pillows, on the floor, and probably even on the wall.

I'm crying. I'm scared. My dad just hit me in front of my best friend and I want to go away. I want to hide. I want to hide. I want to hide.

She wants to go home and I want to go with her. I want to go with her and take Rusty with me. He's the only thing in this house that is nice to me. Besides my Barbies and my Cabbage Patch Kids.

I know that I'll never have her over to my house again. She wants to go home and she'll never come back. And I won't ask her to. She's my best friend and she'll never come over again. I HATE BILL AND I HATE MY MOM!

No one comes in to see if I'm okay. I'm sitting in my blood and my scaredness and I'm a bad girl. That's it. I cry. My blood and my scaredness and I'm a bad girl. I must really be a bad girl.

No one loves me. I'm all alone. My family hates me because I talked back. I didn't mean it in a bad way. I was just trying to make my best friend smile.

I have to watch what I say all the time. I can't be funny. I can't act like my friends act around their families. I can't do what my friends do, cuz I get hit if I do. I have to be scared and not say wrong things ever. I must really be bad. My mom and dad don't love me. My brother hates me.

I'm really, really bad.

A bad girl.

THIRTEEN YEARS OLD

I stare in the mirror. I see this pretty yet so fucking ugly person staring back. I'm fat. Fat and disgusting. I'm a cow. No one wants me. I'm absolutely gross.

I'm so furious. RAGEful. Vengeful. I hate myself. I'm so gross. Look at my fat, fat, fat thighs. I hate myself.

Why can't I be thin? I want to be skinny. If I were skinny, all of my problems would be gone. I would be happy. I know I would be happy because then I wouldn't care about my fat and guys would like me. All the guys I want want the girls who are skinny. I'm disgusting.

RAGE! RAGE! RAGE!

I need to hurt something. I need to do something.

I look into the shower. There's a razor. That'll do what I need right now. I need to hurt something. Cut something. I grind my teeth. I am so furious. I hate my body. I'm a disgusting pig. RAGE! RAGE! RAGE!

All I think about is that I need to do something now to fulfill the RAGE.

I grab the razor. Can I do this? Where should I do it? I just want to see some blood. I want to see blood. All I need is some blood. Blood and pain is all I can think about. Blood and pain. Blood and pain.

My mom is on the other side of the wall, in the kitchen. We live in a shoebox so I have to be quiet. As long as I'm quiet she won't know. She doesn't notice anything that I do anyway. She doesn't notice me. She only notices that I'm fatter than she is. "BIG" is what she always calls me. She only notices her boyfriends. Men. All she gives a shit about is men. Men are her razor. Men are her blood. Men are her pain.

I pull up the sleeve of my left arm. Can I do this? I'm fat and disgusting. Of course I can do this. I need the blood and the pain. I need it like I have never needed anything before. I am desperate.

I slice my wrist lightly with the razor. Not to draw blood. Just to get a taste of the beautiful pain. It hurts a little, but not enough.

This time I slice deeper. I clench my fist and dig my fingernails into my palm. This time there is blood. This time there is pain. I am hot. I am flushed. I feel sweat on my face and adrenaline in my veins. This next time I need to go deeper and then I'll move on to the next arm.

I've been in the bathroom for at least ten minutes now and my mom still hasn't noticed. No water running. No toilet flushing. You would think she would notice, but she doesn't. She's thinking of her man again. That's all she gives a shit about. If she did knock, what would I say? I wish she would knock. I hope she doesn't knock.

I know she won't knock.

This time I push the razor the deepest yet. I slice over the already open, bloody flesh. It STINGS. It STINGS! Fuck. FUCK! FUCK! It stings like I've never felt. I can't do this anymore. I can't go on to the next arm. I can't get it to stop bleeding. I can't stop the bleeding on this arm. I wrap it in toilet paper and push down hard. As the toilet paper hits the open flesh it STINGS. It stings like someone has just poured alcohol into it.

I keep pushing down on it. I need to stop the bleeding so that I can do the other arm . . . I'm grinding my teeth again. The RAGE is back. I'm furious. I need more. I have to cut more. I can't cut more. This is hard work. This is something that I shouldn't be doing. Why the hell am I doing this? I don't understand. What is wrong with me? What is wrong with me? What the hell is wrong with me?!?!?

As I press the toilet paper on my wrist I look down and get a glance at my disgusting thighs. I want to cut them off. I want to cut the fat off of the inside of my thighs. I am repulsively fat and disgusting. GROSS! I AM SO FUCKING GROSS!

Look at yourself. Look at the fat on your ankles. You can't even see your anklebones because you are so fat. You are huge. You are nasty. You are BIGger than every girl you know. You need to cut the fat off of your thighs. NOW!

But I can't. I'm too much of a sissy. I am a BIG, fucking, fat sissy. I can't even cut myself right.

What is wrong with you? You are a BIG, fucking, fat sissy. You can't even cut yourself right. Just do it, you sissy. Cut the fat off of your thighs. That's the only way you are going to feel better. You have to slice the fat off of your thighs so that you will be skinny and happy. If you were skinny, you fat ass, you would be happy. You are such a fucking idiot.

I ignore the voice. I can't bring myself to do it. I can't cut my thighs. I can't do it. I'm a BIG, fucking, fat sissy.

I go back to my wrist.

It's time for the other wrist. I pull the sleeve up. I do the same thing that I did on the left wrist. I slice the top few layers of skin first. No fingernails digging into my hand on that one. It's not deep enough yet. I'm too chicken shit to go all the way on the first slice.

This time I go deeper. I feel the sweat on my face. My whole body feels as if I were sprayed with hot mist. I feel flushed. The blood rushes to my face as I see the blood rise to the surface of the slice. Blood. I see the blood. I need the blood.

I go in again. I go deeper. This time it stings so bad that my arm twitches. Lots of blood rushes. Rushes to the surface. I stare at it. I grit my teeth. I clench my jaw. It's bright red. Not like the fat on my thighs. It's clean. It's pure. It's not nasty like the fat on my thighs.

It comes up and has nowhere to go but down the side of my wrist.

I grab the toilet paper and sit on the toilet and wrap my wrist with it.

STINGS. STINGS. STINGS.

As the paper sits on the slices, I see the blood coming to get me. It doesn't want me to stop. It's telling me to look at it. It says APPRECIATE ME, DAMN IT! YOU'RE THE ONE WHO WANTED ME TO COME OUT AND DANCE ON YOUR WRIST! LOOK AT ME!

I sit on the edge of the toilet and stare at my wrists wrapped in blood-stained paper and think to myself. I think. I berate. I condemn.

What's wrong with me? What's wrong with me? Why did I just do that? I try to figure it out. Nothing. Nothing. Nothing comes to mind except that I am a pathetic little brat who needed to know that I can hurt myself. I am such a loser. I am a fat loser who is too much of a sissy to cut the fat off my thighs.

I only did the wrists because I was too much of a sissy to cut the fat off my disgusting thighs.

It was the easy way out.

EIGHTEEN YEARS OLD

I'm drunk. I'm drunk again. Stoned too. Smoked lots of pot, but I can't feel it because I am so drunk. I know we're fighting, but I have no idea why or what about.

We're in our tiny, filthy, cockroach-infested apartment downtown. My first apartment ever. It's small and crowded and I love it because it's mine. Oh, and Sean's. Sean is my boyfriend. I've had a crush on him since I was thirteen years old and he was dating my best friend Ramie's sister, Autumn.

Autumn is a bitch. She always has been. She's hated me from the moment I met her. I have no idea why. I've never been anything but nice to her. She's very popular and pretty. Exotic looking. Her mom is Native American and her dad was adopted. He looks Asian. All of the girls in Ramie's family are pretty, but especially Autumn. She's got jet black hair and beautiful black-brown eyes. She's thin and dark and what every man wants. I wish I looked like her. My friends tell me she hates me because she's jealous of me. I don't believe them. She has no reason to be jealous of me; I'm disgusting.

Ramie tells me she hates me because I kiss her ass. I don't believe that either. Autumn hated me before I ever said one word to her. I tried being nice to her and she went out of her way to hate me. She's just a bitch. She's a total fucking bitch. I don't understand why she never liked me.

Autumn and Sean dated for two years. He got her pregnant. They got an abortion. We'll last longer than that. He loves me more than he did her and that'll prove it.

We're yelling at each other. Sean and me. I have no idea what about. This happens almost every time we get into a fight. We scream and yell. Sometimes he shoves me. Sometimes he grabs me. But he never hits me. I wouldn't be with a guy who hits me. I'm not my mom.

The apartment is set up just like a hotel room, except that there's a kitchen attached. We're standing in front of the bathroom sink. He's pissed. He's really angry. I must've said something to really piss him off because he shoves me into the bedroom.

I hit the floor. He grabs the mattress off of the bed and throws it on top of me. He puts all of his strength into smashing me under it. He has this look in his eyes. He always has that look like he wants to kill something when he's pissed. He wants to hurt me. That's his goal when he's got that look in his eyes. Hurt. Punish. Humiliate.

I start to cry. Everything is blurry. I'm crying. But I'm furious. I love him. Why is he doing this to me? I don't understand. What did I do?

I'm furious. I'm fucking furious. RAGE. RAGE. RAGE. I feel the Rage welling up inside of me. Fuck him! FUCK HIM!

I get up. I say something to taunt him.

He comes after me again. This time he grabs me in the bathroom in front of the mirror. He grabs me from behind. He has his arms around my ribcage. We're facing the mirror. He looks into the mirror with that look. That look. Hurt. Punish. Humiliate. He wants to hurt me. He has a tight grip around my ribs. I can barely breathe. I have a hard time breathing. He's a constrictor.

The corners of his lips curl into a sadistic smile. Our eyes lock in the mirror. He is laughing at me through the smile. He is laughing at me. He hates me. He wants to see me punished.

He starts to squeeze. He squeezes harder and tighter. Tighter. Tighter. I can't breathe. His smile turns into the determined, raging expression of a lunatic.

I'm seeing spots. I can't breathe. My ribs are crushing. Crushing. Fucking crushing!

POP!

I cry out in pain and he drops me to the ground.

No apology. No checking to see how I am. No nothing. He was finished.

He hurt. He punished. He humiliated.
He was done.

TEN YEARS OLD

I hear cheering. The others are all playing a game. Some kind of birth-day game.

I'm under a blanket with a boy named Chase. His fingers are in my pants. He has his fingers inside of me. He is kissing me. Wet. Sloppy. Disgusting.

The others might hear. Or see. Or come and move the blanket. I'm worried that the others are going to see. If they lift the blanket and see where his hands are, everyone will know I'm dirty.

But he wants to touch me. He likes me. So I'm going to stay under the blanket with him. He didn't want any other girl to come under the blanket with him. He chose me.

His fingers are inside of me. He moves them around. He doesn't touch me like my cousin does. Chase doesn't touch me where it feels good. His fingers just move around. He doesn't know where he can touch me to make it feel good like my cousin does.

I hear the other kids ooh and ahh and giggle about the blanket moving. We're the only ones who aren't playing the game. But I will always be under the blanket before I play a game.

It's my best friend Sage's eleventh birthday. We're in the fifth grade. She's having a party at her house. All of our friends are here from school. Plus some of her friends from her black church in Mis-soula. She doesn't go to the church here because there are no black people.

There are only two black families in our mountain town. Only two. It's very white here. Sage is one of only a few non-white people in our school. It's very white. I don't know why.

My mom always told me to be nice to people, all people. Her mom calls Mexican people "wetbacks" and black people "colored." I think it's weird because we are all colored. She makes jokes that my mom says are "racist." I guess that means that she is mean to black people.

Chase is gross. He's really ugly and I don't think he's cute at all. Not because he's dark skinned, but just because he's not cute and he's always loud. I like a boy named Jonathan. He's really cute.

But Chase wants to touch me.

FIFTEEN YEARS OLD

"HOLY SHIT! THE BED IS BREATHING! RAMIE, GET IN HERE! THE BED IS BREATHING!"

As I stare at the bed, which is moving like a plastic bag that someone is hyperventilating into, Ramie comes in the room. It's my mom's room.

"Look at this! Holy shit! Look at this! The fucking bed is breathing! Do you see that?" She sees it. We stare at the bed for what seems like hours. I don't know how long we actually stare. But we stare. We are fixated. The bed is breathing. We are breathing. We are all one. Me. Ramie. The bed. We are all one.

I am entranced. I am fucking entranced. I am entranced by the bed's inhalation and exhalation. George Washington. Suddenly George Washington is staring back at me. His face is actually in the comforter. It's not flat. It's got bumps and curves and texture to it. He is in the comforter.

Ramie yells, "It's George Washington!"

Yes, yes it is. We stare and giggle. Stare and giggle. Giggle. Giggle. Giggle some more. Life is hilarious. The president is hilarious. Ramie is hilarious. I love my life. I love the blanket. I love being alive!

I turn my head for a brief moment and see the shag carpet. Olive green shag carpet. It has the world in it. It waves hello to me. It dances. It tells me a story. It is my new love.

"Holy shit, Ramie! Look at the carpet!"

Too late. I turn around and Ramie is gone.

I call out, "Ramie! Ramie! Ramie!"

"I'm in here."

I make the walk from my mother's bedroom through the kitchen down the hall and to my room. Each step feels like I'm in slow motion, floating. I am light and alive. Everything I pass glides next to me. The pictures in the hall follow me into the room. Smooth. Forgiving. Velvety. Supple. Easy. I love this feeling. I am in love with life!

I breathe in. Each breath feels like I am drinking in existence. I inhale bigger than I have ever inhaled before. I don't want to miss a silken drop of the drink called BEING.

She's staring at the carpet. Yellow and shaggy. But it looks better than I have ever seen it look. It is utterly amazing. Amazing. Amazing.

Ramie looks up.

She doesn't need to say a word to me. I know that it's time for us to appreciate the yellow shag carpet. I don't even like calling it that. It is a golden dancing pasture. I've never seen anything like it. My bedroom is warm and light and love. It is glowing golden love.

I love being in here. This is where I was meant to be. This is where I come from. This is where it all happens. This is heaven. Heaven in my room. The golden dancing pasture invites me to lie down. I lay down and absorb the blissful drink of BEING. I am here. I have come. I soak it in.

I hear a car. Why do I hear a car? No one is supposed to be home yet.

I jump up. I look out the window and my heart stops. It really stops.

A red pickup truck is in the driveway.

"HOLY SHIT! RAMIE! MY FUCKING MOM IS HOME!!!!!"

FUCK! FUCK! FUCK!

Heaven is gone. BEING is gone. Love is gone. It is all gone. All there is is terror. Panic. Panic. Fear. Dread. Frantic. Mania. Panic.

OH MY GOD! MY MOM IS HOME!

I am frantic. I am crazed. I am so fucked! Oh shit, Ramie.

I look at Ramie and she has no eyes. Just huge, ink-black pupils. She has no fucking eyes, just huge black pupils. The pupils, the huge black pupils have swallowed the brown. Her eyes have no brown. The pupils stretch out to her eyebrows. She has no eyes. Just pupils.

I run to my mirror.

OH FUCK! I have no eyes. The ink-black has swallowed the blue. Where is the blue? Where is the blue? I need the blue. I have to have the blue.

My mom is going to take one look at me and know. *She knows.* She knows about the pupils swallowing the eyes. Her eyes have been swallowed before. She's had the brown stolen from her eyes by the ink-black. She fucking knows.

My mom steps out of her truck. She looks like a fucking clown. Her afro is bigger than I've ever seen it. She has no head. Just a huge, fake-ass-blonde afro. Her afro is coming to get us. What are we going to do? Ramie?

We have to pack. We have to get our shit together. We have to tell her we are going swimming at the recreation center and pack. We have to get our shit together and go. We have to go. We have to get our shit together. She's going to know. How are we going to get out of here?

Okay . . . I can do this. I open my drawer and grab two swimsuits and throw them in my backpack. I hear the front door open. Oh my God, my fucking God! She's in. She's here. She's going to know. She knows. She's had her eyes swallowed before.

No, I can do this. I have to. Get out alive. Just get out as quick as I can without her knowing. That's all I have to do. That's all I have to do.

"Arabella, I'm home."

"Okay, Mom."

Oh my God, did that sound obvious? She can tell by my voice that something is wrong.

"What's up?"

"We're just hanging out in my room. We're getting ready to go swimming."

"Okay."

I run into the hall while she's in her room changing out of her work clothes. I grab two towels. We can get out while she's in her room. YES! We have an escape.

We rush to the front door and just as I pull it open and step onto the porch, her bedroom door opens.

"Did you do your chores?"

I don't look at her. She's on a mission. She walks over to the fridge.

"Yeah, I did 'em. Okay, bye."

She opens the fridge. "You didn't make a salad."

OH MY FUCKING GOD! I didn't make the salad. I CANNOT make a salad right now.

"Oh, I'll do it when I get back, Mom. I'll be back in a couple hours."

Kamie's on the porch. She looks at me with desperation. Her pupils say FUCK!

Fuck! Please. Please. Please. Please let her let me make the salad when I get back.

"When are you coming back?"

"We'll be back in a couple of hours."

She looks at me but I act like I am looking at Ramie for an idea of when I'll be back.

She knows. I know she knows. Her eyes have been stolen before. She knows that I'm hiding something.

"No, make a salad before you go."

My life is over. My heart stops again. I can't do this. I am panicked. I can't do this. I cannot make a salad in front of her. She knows. My life is over. I'm never going to see Ramie again. She thinks that Ramie is a bad influence. She will never let me see her again.

"Okay."

I have no choice. I set down my backpack and walk to the fridge.

Ramie beelines to my room. I hear her buzz with panic. She knows I am dead. I hear her thoughts. You are dead. You are dead. The bedroom door shuts.

My mom is at the sink. She is washing her hands. I run to the fridge. Nothing is floating along with me. There is no Gliding. There is no Smooth. No Forgiving. No Velvety. Nothing Supple. Nothing Easy. Only Panic that she knows. That she will see that I have no eyes.

I kneel down and reach into the fridge and grab the goods for the salad. I grab the celery and notice that it's wilted. It's covered in brown slime. It's floppy in my hand.

In horror I say, "Oh my God, what's wrong with this *lettuce?*"

From behind me I feel my mom turn around and look at the celery. She says, "What are you talking about? That's *celery*. There's nothing wrong with the celery."

I look back down. The celery is fine. Oh shit. I had said "lettuce," not "celery," and I thought that it was wilted.

I say, "Oh, I guess it just looked brown for a minute there."

I know she knows. She hasn't said anything yet, but I know that she knows. She has to know. I freaked out over the celery. Get it together. I have to get it together. GET IT TOGETHER, ARABELLA!

Everything is swirling around me. I feel panic. The fridge is freezing. I manage to pull out all of the salad goods from the fridge and set them on the counter. I get the cutting board. I get the butcher knife.

It's huge. The fucking butcher knife is huge. God, please don't let me cut my fingers off. My hands are shaking. Can she see them shaking? I hope she can't see them shaking. She can see them shaking. She knows. I'm acting like a freak. She knows my hands are shaking.

I start to pull the goods out of their bags. I start to rinse the vegetables. As I rinse the newly revived celery, I look out the window. It's sunny out. It's always sunny here. It's also raining out. Sprinkling when it's sunny. That's normal.

"Look, Mom. It's raining out."

My mom is standing next to me doing something that I don't care about. She looks outside, looks at me, and says, "No it's not."

Again I try to cover my ass and say, "Oh, it just looked like it was for a second there."

"Arabella, *what is wrong with you?*" she asks.

I am fucked Iamfuckedlamfuckedfucked! FUCKING FUCKED!

"Nothing's wrong. It just looked like it was raining for a minute. It must've been the way the light was shining."

She stares at me. Comes close and demands, "Look at me!"

I think about looking up. Fuck. I'm dead. I am so dead. She knows something. She can see that my eyes are stolen. She can see it all. She knows the truth. She is The Punisher.

I have to look up. I look up. I look into her eyes. But I don't see her eyes. I see her fucking clown hair break dancing on her head. I see her ridiculous, fucking clown hair. Her fake, fake, fake, bleach-blonde afro jumping around on her head. There should be music. Her afro has rhythm.

"What are you on? Have you been drinking?"

"No!"

Shit, that was obvious. I sounded so defensive. She barely even got the fucking words out of her mouth before I blurted out no. I am so fucked. She knows.

She stares at me. I am uncomfortable. I am scared. Visibly uncomfortable. She may as well be a fucking mass murderer. I am that scared. Panic. She knows. God, I'm dead. She fucking knows.

"You're acting weird. Let me smell your breath."

SIX YEARS OLD

It's dark in here. I wish Rusty was down here with me. I want to sleep with him. I don't know why he always gets to sleep with him. He just likes me to be alone. Everyone in this house likes me to be alone. They don't like me. My mom don't like me. Bill don't like me. And my big brother, Dave, don't like me either.

I wish it was light out. I don't like the dark. I really don't like being in here when the door is shut. At least my big brother is in the top bunk. If I was alone I'd be scareder.

He whispers, "Arabella, are you awake?"

I just lie here. I just lie here because he is probably going to say something mean to me. He is always mean. Never nice. He hates me because I'm littler than him and he is bigger than me. I always ruin his fun cuz he has to babysit me.

He makes me cry a lot. He makes fun of the way I say my name. I can't say my r's right so he makes fun of me. He thinks it's funny that I can't say my r's. And there's an r in my name, so I have to say it a lot. This is the only house that I remember where I can't say my r's right.

He whispers again, "Arabella are you awake?"

This time I whisper back. "What?"

"Come up here and pet the kitty."

"Why?"

"Just come up here and pet the kitty."

"Why?"

"Just do it."

I don't feel good all of a sudden. Dave is never nice to me. Why does he want me to come up to the top bunk with him and pet Rusty? I feel scared all of a sudden. I don't want to go up to his bunk and pet the kitty. I feel the same feeling in my tummy that I feel when my cousin tells me not to tell anyone. I don't want to go up there with my big brother.

"No. I don't want to. You pet Rusty. I don't want to."

"Come on, just come pet him."

I'm scared again. I want to go tell my mom. Or tell Bill. But then Dave will beat me up when they go to work. I can't ever tell on him cuz then he punches me when they go to work.

I'm scared. I'm scared. I'm scared.

Go away. Go away. Go away. Go away.

Please leave me alone.

FOURTEEN YEARS OLD

I wake up to a voice.

"Bella, come here."

The blue and white lights flickering from the TV shine on Ramie's sleeping face.

"Bella, come here."

Oh Jesus. What the fuck? I turn to see my cousin Matt squatting next to my pillow.

I know what he wants.

FLASH!

I'm in Otis again. My mom has decided that she wanted us to come back and visit my grandpa before he dies. He's dying. I'm not even really sure of what. He's paralyzed and he can barely speak. I'm afraid to be around him. I'm afraid I won't be able to understand him. I'm afraid that I'll start crying.

I've been avoiding him since we got here. I'm bad. I'm fucking bad. But I can't see him. He lays in the living room in his hospital bed and watches TV. He also watches me walk in and out of the house. He watches me ignore him.

As I walk past him I don't stop to sit at his side. My mom is by his side a lot. My grandma is always by his side. My brother sits at his side too. I'm the only one who doesn't. I'm afraid of him. I'm afraid of him and I don't know why. I am such a fucking asshole. I'm so selfish. I am terrible. I'm afraid of my grandpa. My grandpa! The only man who never once laid a hand on me. The only man who never once said anything mean to me. I am afraid of him. I am awful.

My mom asks me why I don't say hello to him. I tell her I don't know, but I don't talk to her about it. I learned a long time ago that I can't tell her stuff. She is not to be trusted . . .

"Bella, come here."

He whispers louder this time. I know what he fucking wants. The only thing that he ever wants from me. I used to get excited about it. I used to feel special and wanted and pretty. Wanted. Now, I am furious. Livid. Irate. FUCKING FURIOUS!!

I grind my teeth. I fucking hate him. I hate this. I HATE THIS! I FUCKING HATE THIS!

Ramie is going to wake up and see. Then she's going to know that my cousin fucks me. She is going to find out that I am some disgusting white-trash, cousin-fucking whore.

GET THE FUCK AWAY FROM ME, I want to scream. I have to get him away from me. I have to get him away from me. I have to get him to leave me alone before Ramie finds out. Leave me alone you fucking asshole!

That's what I want to say, but instead I say, "No. Leave me alone."

"Come on. Come into the bedroom. Come into the bedroom, Bella."

His whispering is louder. I look at Ramie. She's still sleeping. But she won't be for long if he keeps at it.

I fucking hate this. LEAVE ME ALONE! Goddamn it! What the fuck did I do to deserve this? Leave me alone! I wish I could scream! I want to scream! I want to punch him in the face. I want to kick him in the stomach. All there is is RAGE. RAGE. FUCKING RAGE!

"Come on, Bella. Come into the bedroom."

He is touching my arm now. His persistence is growing.

"Come on! Come in the bedroom with me, pleeease."

His fucking s's hiss like a snake. He is a snake and I am his dinner. He wants to eat me for dinner. I am just prey to him. I am not a person. I am only what he needs to fill himself up. But first he must squeeze the life out of me. He must wear me down. He must drain me like they all do. Get what they want from me. Take. Take. Take. I am just here to have the life squeezed out of me. Everyone constricts.

He knows if he wears me down enough, I will lie lifeless and submit. He just has to wear me down and then he can have me for dinner.

"Come on. Come into the bedroom."

Again his hiss gets louder.

I tell him again to leave me alone. "Please," I hiss back this time, "leave me alone. Ramie is going to see."

He is relentless. He knows that if he stays and hisses long enough, I will eventually become lifeless. He will have his meal.

I look over at Ramie. I am so disgusting. I can't believe that I have sex with my cousin. I am so sick. I am so wrong. I am so fucked up. I am a slut. A cousin-fucking slut. RAGE! FURY! MADNESS!

I want to hurt someone right now. I hate myself. I am so disgusting and I hate him. I hate him for making me his slave. I hate him for making me want his attention when I was young. I hate him for making my body respond—

SNAP!

Something takes over my body. The Rage is gone. Resolve has set in.

I have to do this. There is no other option. I have to do it and then he'll go away. I have to do this and then he'll go away. If I get it over with he will leave me alone. Then I will have peace. There is no other way. If I keep saying no, he will never leave. He will wake up Ramie. Then Ramie will know that I am a cousin-fucking whore. She will know that I am disgusting. She will know why I hate myself so much. Why I am so bad. She will know the truth. She will hate me. I have to do what he says to get this moment over with. If I do what he says it will be over. Do what he says. Do what he says. Do what he says.

I will have peace when it is all over with. I will have peace when it is all over with. Peace. Peace. Peace.

I get up and follow him into the bedroom.

My body is there. I don't know where my mind is. Half of it is floating away somewhere else. Fantasies of peace and bliss. Fantasies of it being over. Over. Peace. Alone. Calm. Bliss. Gone. Gone. Gone.

The other half of my mind is consumed with worry that Ramie or my aunt or uncle or cousins will walk in and find out that I am a BIG whore. They will know and my life will be over. My life will be over. They will know that I have committed incest. I have committed the most disgusting sin of all. Incest.

But we're not blood-related.

TWENTY-TWO YEARS OLD

Palm Beach

"Suck my dick, bitch! I bought you drinks all night and now you're going to suck my dick."

That's all I hear. That's all I see. Over and over again.

FLASH!
"Suck my dick, bitch!"

FLASH!
"Suck my dick, bitch!"

FLASH!
I'm in the corner.
I'm on my knees.
His fat, hard, disgusting cock is in my mouth.

FLASH!
"Get the fuck out of here you slut!"

FLASH!
"Get the fuck out you fucking slut!"

FLASH!
I'm wandering the streets, shit-faced.

FLASH!
I'm lost in a city I don't know.
I'm a whore. I'm a slut. I don't know where I am. I don't know where I am. I don't know where the fuck I am!
But I know that I am a slut . . .

I roll over and stare at the hotel curtain and wonder how I made it to my room last night. How I found my way home from his hotel room. How I got here.
I need a drink. Now.

SIXTEEN YEARS OLD

"WHAT THE FUCK IS WRONG WITH YOU, ARABELLA?"

I just stare. I'm in a fucking hospital and I just stare through the BLUR of what just happened.

The vodka is starting to wear off and all I feel is pain. My head is throbbing like it has never throbbed before. I can't stand this. I need water. I need sleep. I need to take back the past five hours.

"What the fuck is wrong with you? My dad is going to fucking kill you! Your mom is going to fucking kill you!"

Yeah, I fucking know they're going to kill me, you stupid fucking bitch. I know I'm dead. I want to tell her that but I don't.

Instead, I say, "I know."

I know. I'm fucked. I feel only shame. Pain. Excruciating. Overwhelming. Pain. Pain. Pain. My head is throbbing. Pounding. Thudding. I know this feeling better than any other.

She is yelling at me in the hospital. I am embarrassed because she's yelling. I'm embarrassed because she's drunk. I'm embarrassed because she has a birth defect and she sounds like she's fucking retarded.

Everyone in the fucking hospital thinks I'm being yelled at by a fucking retard. My head is splitting and I'm being yelled at by a fucking retard. Fucking great.

Her friend is standing next to her. They hate me. I can see it in their eyes. They think I'm a fucking loser. I've seen this friend before. She's seen me drunk. She's seen me stupid. She looks at me with disgust. I am better off dead. Everyone hates me.

BLUR.

"My dad let you use his truck while they are gone!"

BLUR.

"And *this* is what you do?!? You fucked it all up!"

BLUR.

YELL. YELL. YELL.

"HE WAS GOING TO GIVE YOU THAT TRUCK IF YOU DID GOOD WITH IT WHILE THEY WERE GONE! YOU SO FUCKED UP!"

All I hear is, "Fuck-up." Yelling. That's all I hear. I can't focus on anything. I can't focus on anything but her blurry, retarded yelling and the throbbing in my head. Pounding. Pounding. Thudding. Berating. Condemning. Cursing. Hating. Killing.

I wish I was dead. I wish I was dead. Then all of this would be gone. I wish I was dead. God, please take me now. Please, Please, Please. I want to die. I want to disappear. Please, make me disappear God.

My name should be changed to Fuck-up.

SIXTEEN YEARS OLD

"Are you sure you're okay to drive?"

"I'm fine."

"Are you sure? Because you can stay here tonight."

"Nah, I have to go. I'm fine to drive."

The truth is I don't want to be there. I don't know what time it is, but I know it's after midnight.

I'm at my good friend Amy's house. Her parents are upstairs sleeping. Actually, chances are they are passed out drunk. We could steal—and have stolen—half a bottle of hard liquor and they'd never know the difference.

I've just got to get out of here. Amy is dating Ryan. I can't stand being around them anymore. I can't take anymore tonight.

I've had a crush on Ryan for a long time. He's a year older than me and I think that he's really hot. I don't know much about him. I've gotten high with him a lot though. He's gorgeous and Amy is with him. Amy always gets the guys I like. Guys love Amy because she is stunningly beautiful. I wish I were her. She is gorgeous. She is petite and cute. She has emerald green eyes and full, flowing brown hair. She is what every guy wants. She has everything that the guys that I like want. I wish I were her.

I am nothing compared to her. I am huge. I am BIG. If I were skinny and pretty like her, I would be happy. Why couldn't I look like her? Why couldn't I have really rich parents? Why couldn't I have a truck given to me when I turned sixteen? I wish I were her. I fucking hate being me. I hate being me. I hate being me.

I can't take this anymore. I can't watch the guy I like make out with my perfect friend. I have to go.

I jump in the truck. I turn the ignition. I go.

I leave the place where my perfect friend has gotten my perfect guy. He is supposed to be with me. But I'm not perfect, so he's with Amy instead.

My mom's boyfriend, Daryl, told me I could borrow the truck while they are in Las Vegas. They always go on trips without my brother and me. My mom disappears for the weekends to visit him on his hiking trips. He's a mountain guide. In the summer. In the winter he's a ski instructor. They're always out having fun. Without me.

It's fine with me. My brother and I just throw parties while she's gone. Well, we used to until she was notified by all of the neighbors. Now we have to go to our friends' houses, or we just park the cars down the road, sneak into the house, and shut the drapes. We do drugs and drink. Lots. Well, I do drugs.

My brother thinks drugs are for losers. He's just a big fucking drunk. Apparently *alcoholics* aren't losers. I think he's a loser with or without the booze. He's an asshole. Always has been. A fucking asshole. I fucking hate my brother.

I don't know where to go. I can't go home. I'm not supposed to be there. I'm supposed to be at Daryl's daughter's house. She's got a birth defect so she talks fucked up, but there's nothing wrong with her mentally. Just physically. Her boyfriend has stacks of porno magazines right next to where I am supposed to sleep. Nice.

I have to go there. I can make it. All I have to do is drive down the canyon where the cops won't be. Drive down the canyon and I'll be near

Missoula. Then it's all highway from there. I just have to drive for another forty minutes and I'll be there.

I'm tired. I can do this. I can do this. I can do this. I am awake.

I open the window for air, turn up the stereo. I only have a little way to go. I can make it. Just through the canyon and I'm there. I can do this. Canyon. Canyon. Canyon . . .

Suddenly, my eyes jerk open. I'm upside-down.

RRRRREEEEEEEEEEECCCCCCCCCCCHHHHHHHHHH!

What the fuck is happening? I see sparks. Sparks fly everywhere. Huge sparks! And there's the loudest screeching noise I have ever heard in my life. It sounds like someone is scraping a butcher knife against a metal pipe. It sounds like something from a movie. One of those movies where a semitruck is sliding upside-down on the highway because it just flipped over. Sparks are flying everywhere. It's like the Fourth of July, only upside-down.

I don't know what to do or what is happening. I am upside-down and the truck is scraping across the road and sparks are shooting all around my face and I am confused and scared and lost.

There is no windshield. It's completely gone. The roof is in front of me. It's caved in right in front of my face.

The screeching stops. I hear the river. I hear the river really close. Rushing. Screaming. Gasping. Taunting.

My head is pressing against the roof of the truck. My head is throbbing because I am upside-down and my head is pressing against the roof of the truck.

I have to get out. Get out. Get out now!

I reach down for my seat belt and unhook it. All of my weight goes onto my head. Onto the roof. My head throbs. Throbs and aches and swells with blood. Thin, thin, vodka-infused blood.

I turn to my left and look at the truck door. There's no fucking window. I pull myself out of the window and into the ink-black darkness of the canyon—the cold, dark canyon—and I am all alone.

I am alone as I look at Daryl's truck laying upside-down on the edge of the road, feet from the river.

OH FUCK! WHAT THE FUCK DID I DO?!?!? FUCK! FUCK! FUCK!

I am fucked. I am so fucked. I am so fucked. I am so fucking fucked.

I am alone and fucked.

ELEVEN YEARS OLD

"Arabella, act like you're kissing me."

"No, Mom."

"Come on, it'll be funny."

She's drunk again. Her breath smells like vodka and minty cigarettes. After she smokes in the garage, she comes in and sticks the gum in her mouth that she was chewing before she went out to smoke. Her breath smells like vodka-flavored mint cigarettes.

That's all she drinks. Vodka. First she puts ice cubes in her bright pink plastic cup. Then she pours in the vodka. Sometimes she uses a little glass to measure it out. Sometimes she just pours it straight into the cup. She always eyes it to make sure that she's got enough. She usually takes it with her in the car at night.

She mixes it with orange juice or cranberry juice. If she doesn't have any of that left, she uses water. It smells so gross. Disgusting. I can smell it from across the room. It makes me gag. I feel like I have to puke when I smell it.

I especially hate it on her breath. Her breath smells like it every night.

She pulls me into the living room in front of our huge mirror. It covers half the wall. It sits right above our couch. She thinks it would be funny if she dips me and kisses me like they do in the movies.

She wants it to really look like a movie kiss, so she dips me and puts her hand over her mouth and moves her head around like she's French-kissing me, the way she kisses my dad. This is so annoying. So gross. So wrong.

She's my best friend, but she's so annoying sometimes.

She laughs.

Loud. Annoying. Obnoxious. Annoying. Annoying. Annoying. She has the most annoying laugh in the world. When she laughs, everyone turns to see who the annoying, loud laugh is coming from. I hate being in public with her. She is so embarrassing.

She does it for attention. She always wants to be noticed. Even if it is because she's annoying. She doesn't care.

She dips me again and again and laughs in the mirror. The first time I thought it was kind of funny, I guess. Now it's just annoying.

When she grabs me to kiss me I smell the vodka on her breath and the smoke in her hair. The smoke isn't minty in her hair. Only in her gum.

"Let's go show your dad."

"No, Mom. I don't want to."

"Come on, it'll be funny."

"No. I don't want to."

She grabs my arm and starts to walk me downstairs.

Bill—I mean my dad—is sitting on the couch watching TV.

"We want to show you something funny, Bill."

Oh *God,* I am so embarrassed. Uncomfortable. Shamed. I feel shame. I feel like an idiot. Why does she have to do this to me? How is this funny?

I hate being around him and I hate that she is making me do this. I hate that she wants me to do this for him. For him. For her!

Bill looks up from the TV.

"What?"

I can't even look at him. I beg my mom with my eyes not to make me do this.

She doesn't care. Selfish. Selfish. Selfish. It's all about her. I don't matter at all. It's all about her.

"You ready?"

I think, No! I don't want to do this.

I say, "I guess."

"Okay, Bill, watch this. *Bill?* Watch. Make sure you watch."

"Okay, I'm watching."

She grabs me and dips me and puts her hand over my mouth right before she kisses me. She moves her head around like she's French-kissing my dad.

It lasts forever. I just want this to be over. This is so embarrassing. So totally embarrassing.

It feels like an hour has passed and we're still kissing. And Bill is watching. I don't know how much time has gone by, but it feels like forever. Forever. Forever. I hate this. I hate her. She is so stupid.

It's over.

"What'd you think? Wasn't that funny Bill?"

No, Mom, it wasn't funny at all. Why do you always have to embarrass me? Why do you always have to be the center of attention?

I think these things but I don't say them.

EIGHTEEN YEARS OLD

"Alright; two more questions and we're done."

"Okay," I say.

I'm so nervous. I don't have anything to worry about, but I'm nervous. I've never been hooked up to a lie detector machine before. Just the fact that I'm hooked up to this thing is enough to make me nervous enough that I'll seem like I'm lying. I'm not.

"Have you ever received money for sex?"

Quick scan of my brain.

"No."

That's not a lie. I never have taken money for sex. I'd be rich if I had.

Pause. He eyeballs the machine. I'm looking straight. Forward. I'm supposed to look straight and forward and not move. But I can tell that he's looking at the machine every time I answer a question.

I feel guilty even though I haven't done anything wrong. I feel like he thinks I'm lying even though I'm not. I feel like that a lot. I feel like people think I'm lying when I'm telling the truth. I think I look guilty. I feel guilty.

What am I doing here? Seriously, I can't believe I am actually in here. What am I doing? Why am I here? I'm so nervous. Shit, I can feel sweat on my chest. On my stomach. On the back of my thighs. Sweat. Hot. Nervous.

"Okay, last question. Have you ever charged anyone for sex?"

I pause. I think, Well, I was going to, but the police made it hard for me. So, I guess that's a no.

"No."

"Okay, Arabella. We're done. I'll unhook you from the machine."

He unhooks me, takes the strap off my chest and the clamp off of my finger.

"I'll be back in a couple of minutes."

He takes the test results with him.

I sit and think.

I start with how I showed up here this morning.

Sean doesn't know. He would not be happy if he knew I was here. He wouldn't be happy at all.

FLASH!

I pull up in the parking lot. The single-story building has no windows. There's no name on it, but there are numbers and they're the ones I'm looking for. Only people who know what they're looking for would come here.

I walk in the door. There are dark red lights and two couches. I'm scared. What the hell am I doing here? Oh fuck! What the hell am I getting myself into?

I look around. I feel like I'm in a whorehouse. This is a fucking whorehouse. What am I doing here? I look over to the couches and there are three women sitting on the couches. One is wearing a bright green thong and no top. She has a perfect body. She is better than me. What am I doing here? I'm not good enough to be here.

The other is wearing a lacy pink negligee and she has her hair done up like Dolly Parton. She looks like Dolly Parton. She's really pretty. Her boobs are springing out of her top. Her makeup is on so thick she'll need a chisel to get it off tonight. She's better than me. She is so sexy.

There's another one who has on a tiny black mini-skirt and a sheer top with a bra underneath. She's better than me. She's absolutely gorgeous. She looks like Autumn. She is perfect.

There's a window cut out of the wall and there's a big fat man and a short blonde woman inside. The blonde woman looks like she's still living in the '80s. Her hair's bleach-blonde and she has bangs that go halfway back the top of her head.

She takes me into one of the rooms.

There's a hot tub in the room. There is a hot tub in every room. The door shuts and you get naked in the tub with the guy. He is allowed to touch only your breasts—if you want him to. You'll get better tips. You can touch yourself, but you cannot touch him—AT ALL.

Most guys will masturbate looking at you.

She shows me the little white hand towels that are for cum. The men aren't allowed to cum in the hot tub.

"Do you have any questions?"

I say, "No."

I'm too uncomfortable.

I can't think right now. I can't think about anything except how unbelievably uncomfortable I am with the fucking hot tub and the image of disgusting, fucking, beating-off men.

There will be disgusting men beating off to me. In front of me. Maybe even on me. And I have to act like I like it. Fuck. Fuck. Fuck.

I can't do this. I need the money. I owe people money. I need money. This is like $500 a week. I can do this. I'll have Candice paid off in a couple of months if I do this. I can do this. I'll have lots of money . . .

I look around the room. It's a giant garage. I was just strapped up to a lie detector machine in a garage at a fucking whorehouse. What the fuck am I doing? I can't do this.

No, I can do this. I can because I need the money.

FLASH!

We're walking in the hallway and an old—and I don't mean Harrison Ford old, we're talkin' Yoda old—Asian guy asks her if he can have me.

He says, "I wah huh. I wah huh."

"No, she's not working here yet."

"When she stah?"

"I don't know when she's going to start. We're still interviewing her."

"Oh, when she stah, I wah huh."

He is fucking disgusting. He's fucking old enough to be my father. I feel fucking nasty. I feel fucking gross. I feel so fucking gross. I am a slut. What am I doing here? What am I doing? *What am I fucking doing?* . . .

The big fat man who interviewed me walks in the garage and sits down across from the lie detector machine where he was when he conducted the test.

I'm nervous. What if the test says that I lied when I didn't?

I told the truth, but I feel like a liar. I feel like he thinks I'm a liar. I always feel like people think that I'm lying. I feel guilty and wrong all the time. The truth doesn't matter.

"Well, Arabella, I went over the results. They're all good except for one section."

Oh shit.

"What section?"

"The last question—'Have you ever charged anyone for sex?'—showed a different bodily response than the others. Why is that? Have you ever charged anyone for sex?"

He stares at me like I'm on trial for murder.

"No. Umm . . ."

Just say it. Tell him. Tell him about your cousin. I can't tell him. He'll think I'm disgusting. He'll think I'm a cousin-fucking whore. I am *so* uncomfortable. I feel like puking and hiding. Hide. Puke. Hide. Puke. Hide. Hide. I want to hide.

"Well, a little while ago my therapist and my parents wanted me to press charges against someone who did sexual stuff to me. But we didn't actually press charges because the cops in that area knew the person and so they weren't really cooperative. I was nervous because I wasn't sure if I should answer yes for almost pressing charges, or no because we didn't."

He stares at me.

I'm uncomfortable. I don't think he believes me. He thinks I'm a fucking prostitute. He thinks I'm a fucking prostitute!

"Oh. Well . . . that's not what I meant when I asked you that."

"What did you mean?"

I meant have you ever charged someone *money* to have sex with you?

"Oh! GOD NO!"

"Well, that's good. But I do have to tell you that you should think hard about getting a job in this business if you've had someone do those things to you. We don't want to see you doing something for the wrong reasons. Have you gotten help for it?"

He was being kind. His eyes were kind. He was softer. He didn't think I was lying. He knew I was telling the truth.

What a relief. He believes me. He's nice. He's not a bad guy. I think I could work for this guy.

"Yeah. I had a therapist growing up."

That was a lie. Yeah, I had a therapist growing up, but all we talked about was my brother's problem with doing what he's told. All the problems in the family at that time were entirely my brother's fault. He was the problem, not my fucking asshole of a dad. Not my drunk of a mother. Dave was the problem. And I was labeled the "family cop." Sometimes we talked about Bill. Rarely.

"Okay, well, we'll call you in the next few days to let you know if you got the job."

A few days later the phone rang.

I got the job. I start on Monday.

NINE TO TWELVE YEARS OLD
House on Bear Street

It's so sunny out and this is so fun. I'm jumping. Higher. Higher. Higher. I love this trampoline. I love this trampoline. I'm gonna do a flip.

I jump high.

I fling my body forward, tuck my head, and do a FLIP!

I want to do a back flip.

I jump high and close my eyes.

I open them as I land on the canvass on my back.

I fly up in the air and hurl my feet over my head.

That was perfect. That one was a really good one. I wish I could do it that way every time.

I hear a car. I look up the hill and see a car turn onto our steep dirt road.

Scooter, our black dog, and Joker, our brown dog, are sunning themselves in the driveway. I love them. They are so cute.

But as they hear the car, they start to get up and get ready for the chase.

They love the chase. They do it every time. Chase. Chase. Chase the car.

I feel the feelings bubbling up inside of me as the car gets closer.

I know what they're going to do. They never listen to me. They are going to do what they know they aren't supposed to and they won't listen to me when I yell at them. They are bad sometimes.

As the car gets near our house they run up next to it. They chase it as fast as they can. They follow it all the way down by the creek and halfway up the hill behind our house.

I yell at them.

"NO! NO! NO! Get back here. SCOOT! JOKE! GET BACK HERE!!"

They don't listen to me. They never listen to me. They are in so much trouble. I'm gonna kill them. KILL THEM!!

As I watch them running back up the road toward the house I feel this feeling inside. I'm so mad. I'm so mad. I am so mad because they are bad. They don't listen to me. No one ever listens to me. They never listen to me.

I feel like I could freak out. I feel like I do sometimes when I'm alone doing chores. I just want to freak out. Throw stuff. Break something. I am so mad. Throw. Break. Freak.

I yell at them as they come running back. I am mad. I look mean. I want to freak out. FREAK OUT! THOSE STUPID BRATS!

Both of them start to hang their heads and their tails go tucked under their butts. They start to walk. They walk slower and slower as they come near me.

Good. They are afraid of me. They deserve this. They don't listen and this is what happens to bad dogs that don't listen.

SMACK! SMACK! SMACK! SMACK!

Scooter tries to get away from me, but I grab his scruff and get him one last time.

SMACK!

BAD DOG!! BAD DOG!!

He whimpers and runs away as soon as I let go of his scruff.

As I turn to find Joker, I take a deep breath and then exhale.

I feel less like freaking out. I don't feel so mad. Less mad. I don't feel so mad. I feel tired. I feel done. I feel tired.

I don't want to jump anymore.

TWENTY-NINE-AND-A-HALF YEARS OLD

I can't stop crying. I sit here in front of my laptop typing and I can't stop crying.

It took me an hour to write the last section. I got up from my seat three times. The last eight lines took me half of that.

FLASH!
Hitting my dogs.

FLASH!
The rage in my small face. In my meek body. In my starving heart.

FLASH!
The fear and pain in their eyes . . .

If only I could go back and take all of that away. I know that I was a child in a very abusive environment, but if I could take it away, I would.

I feel horrible. I feel terrible. My animals are everything to me.

I can't even imagine yelling at my animals, let alone beating them or hitting them.

I cry every time I think of hitting them.

They both died a few years ago. Now I ask them to forgive me. Whenever I think of them I tell them I am so sorry for what I did to them.

I am sorry that I made you afraid of me the way that I was afraid of the people who were supposed to take care of and love me.

I am so sorry that I stole your trust and innocence.

I am so sorry that I hit you for being yourselves.

I am so sorry that I turned my own rage onto you. I didn't have the right to do that.

I am so sorry. I am so sorry. I am so sorry.

You deserved better. Much better.

My heart breaks with every tear that falls as I think of hurting you.

You two loved me. Both of you. Scooter and Joker and our fuzzy friend Rusty were the only creatures in my life that didn't hurt me. And I hurt you. I hurt you despite the fact that neither of you ever did anything but love me.

Anguish. Grief. Regret. Shame. Sorrow.

TWENTY-THREE YEARS OLD

As I sit down I look around.

There are candles burning. There is incense burning. There are little spiritual trinkets everywhere.

I'm nervous. I am so nervous. She's going to see right through me. Why am I even here? She's going to take one look at me and see right through me. She's going to see that I'm a slut. A drug addict. A thief. A liar. A bad person. I am a horrible, bad person. And she's going to see that.

But I need information. I need someone to tell me that everything is going to be okay. I need hope. I need something. I am lost. So lost. SO VERY LOST.

I look across the table at her. I say only hello. She says hello while she lights the incense. She has huge green-blue eyes. She's plump and has long sandy hair. Not at all what I was expecting her to look like. I thought she would be more saintly looking or something. Maybe wearing a silken shawl or flowing skirt or something. She looks ordinary.

"Should we get started?"

"Yes."

"It's $100 for fifteen minutes."

"Okay."

I'm still nervous that she's going to tell me what a horrible person I am. How very terrible I am. She can see right through me and she can see what a worthless person I am.

She hits the record button on the tape recorder. The tape starts to spin.

She begins.

"You, my dear, are a natural-born caretaker. It's in your nature. You have to do this for a living or you'll end up doing it in relationships. To your detriment. You would be excellent in nursing. You don't mind other people's blood. But the sight of your own doesn't work for you."

Wrong there. I don't mind my own blood. I keep this to myself.

"You would be good in any healing profession. I see you excelling at massage. You need to be doing something with your hands. You are a very hands-on kind of person."

Wrong and right. I am a healer. Yes, I know this.

Magic.

I could've done massage had it not been for that fucking car accident. The only massages that will be taking place are the ones that I go to once a week.

"Whatever you do I see you going to school for no more than a year."

She tells me that she hears wedding bells. She says it a few times.

Magic.

I ask her when. And who is this guy? Will I know him when I see him? I am totally stoked about this.

In the next year or two I will meet him. I won't know right away. But he is my soul mate. He is so sweet. He is my soul mate.

Magic.

That's very encouraging.

"How will I meet him?"

"You need to get out and do the things that you love. Go out and find the things that you love. He may have a child from a previous marriage."

Magic.

She looks at me with a depth of seriousness and kindheartedness.

"You need to take that time to do some work on yourself, girlfriend."

Magic.

She smiles and laughs.

"You are so pissed off. You are so angry. You are full of anger. But look how sweet and kind and gentle and loving and giving you are. You're a very sweet and compassionate soul. You help people that other people don't see as worthy of help. You help strangers even when it's inconvenient for you. You are a sweet, gentle soul."

Magic.

I smile. Who, me? Sweet? I thought she was going to tell me what a horrible person I am. Where is she getting this sweet stuff? I certainly don't feel sweet. I feel like a BIG, fat, slutty loser. This feels nice. Hey, I'm sweet.

She's intent again. I am enchanted. Magic swirls around me.

I am hanging on her every word. I know nothing else. She is my goddess right now. She is my everything. She is my oracle. She is my priestess. She is my magician.

She leans in with what I imagine a motherly expression would be like.

"You are going to die if you keep doing drugs . . . you will die."

Magic.

She is dead serious.

I know. I know. I believe you. That's why I stopped. I knew I would die. I almost did die a couple of times. I tell her this. I've been sober for a little over a month. I tell her this.

"You will stay sober. You will succeed at quitting the drugs but I smell cigarettes. You'll start smoking cigarettes again, but you'll stay sober. You will die if you don't. You know you can't keep doing drugs or you will die."

I know.

But that's all the excuse I need to go light up. I can go smoke now. I'm gonna start in the future, so it may as well be now. I think I smell cigarettes too . . . now.

She pauses for a moment and her eyes start to tear up. She looks at me with the most compassion that I've felt from someone in, well, at least many, many years, if ever.

She speaks.

"You don't know what love is. You've never had it. You have never been unconditionally loved by anyone in your whole life. People used you. They hurt you. You don't know what it feels like to be unconditionally loved. Everyone around you used you, abandoned you, or abused you."

Magic. Magic. Magic.

"You were physically abused. I see many kinds of abuse. Honey, I am so sorry."

She pauses and reaches out to place her hand on mine. She says that she is so sorry.

Yeah, you think you're sorry? Fuck. Try living it. I keep that to myself too. But it doesn't matter, because at this point I'm fairly certain she can read my mind.

"I see you having night terrors as a child."

She still has that look of sympathy in her eyes. Compassion. Caring. Gentle. Consideration.

"Oh sweetheart; you were so alone. I see you so alone. And terrified. You never felt safe."

Magic.

That's a fact. I hardly remember NOT feeling terrified. That was the norm. Other feelings were just appendages of the general body of terror. For the first time in my life I feel that someone has felt what I've been through. For the first time in my life my pain is being experienced and validated by another adult. I feel warm and understood. Like Magic.

"You had to take care of yourself. This is one of your biggest lessons in this life. Learning how to take care of yourself. You need to work through your feelings. Stop getting so caught up in trying to forgive and trying to find the good that has been in your life. The fact is there wasn't a whole lot of it and

you need to be angry. You just don't have a whole lot of good to focus on. Unfortunately, it was mostly bad. I'm sorry, but it was. It is not your job to forgive. You don't have to."

Amen to that one, sister. Don't I know it. I hang on her words. She sees me. No one has ever seen me like this.

MAGIC. I want to scream MAGIC! Oh my God, MAGIC!

I interrupt her. "Is my brother okay?"

As I search her eyes for a response, I think about how long he has been missing for. We haven't heard from him in months. He's running from the law. And he's mentally ill. He's tried to kill himself. He's been in a mental hospital. Even though I hate my brother, I am worried about him. Even though part of me wants him dead, the other part of me that is compassionate doesn't. I don't tell her this.

She waits and then says, "He's not in a very good place."

She looks worried.

I ask her point-blank, "Is he going to kill himself?"

"He already is killing himself with the life he's living."

She's reluctant.

I think, Uh, sorry that's not a good enough answer.

"No, is he really going to succeed at killing himself?"

She pauses. She can't decide what she's going to tell me. I see the answer in her eyes.

Just tell me. I need to know.

"His time on this planet is not long. He will try to make things better, but eventually he'll give up. His time on this planet is not long."

Really? Pause. Really?

Even though I am not surprised, I am.

"I'm sorry, sweetie. But that doesn't mean that things can't change. This life is not set in stone. There are many options. Many paths. Things change."

Now I just feel like she's reassuring me. It's a nice gesture, but bullshit—I can tell. I know he'll kill himself. He hates *himself. He's told me more than once. I feel sorry for him when he says stuff like that. Then I remember. Then I remember and I hate him again.*

I need more magic. I need her to see me. ME.

"Do you see me having children?"

I would be a terrible mother. I am no good and I would be a horrible mother, that's why I don't want children. Never. I would not be a good mother. I'm not good enough.

"Yes, there is a little girl who really wants to be in your space. You know why it's a little girl, right?"

She senses my fear.

Yeah.

I give in. I know it. I know it too. Goddamn fucking Magic.

"So that I don't do the same thing that my mom did."

"So that you don't do the same thing that your mom did."

We say this at the same time.

Magic.

"Yes, you are going to be the one to break the cycle."

MAGIC!

I have to break the cycle. I have to break the cycle. I will not be my mother. NO FUCKING WAY! I will not be my mother. My worst nightmare is being my mother.

She looks at me with that same compassionate tenderness and says, "It will be okay. You are going to be so much better than you think you are. So much."

MAGIC . . . MAGIC . . . MAGIC.

This woman doesn't even know me and she sees me. This woman who I don't even know has seen Me. She Sees Me. SHE SEES ME!!

MAGIC. SHE'S MAGIC!

She sees things in me that I can't see. She sees things in me that no one ever saw in me when I was growing up. At least they never told me. This woman has given me hope. This woman has given me hope to hold on for just a little while. I can do this.

She has given me the gift of Magic.

Being Seen is Magic.

THREE TO FIVE YEARS OLD

"You two stay here and I'll be right back."

Mommy walks off with a big guy.

I think I am four years old, but I do not know. My mommy just left me and Davie in the park. She is coming back soon.

Davie is more than two years older than me. He is big. I think he will watch me, but I am still scared.

We play. It is getting worser to see.

"Davie, I am scared. When is Mommy coming back?"

"Mom is coming. Don't worry. She'll be back soon. Just keep playing."

Davie don't look right. He tells me not to worry, but he looks bad. He don't look good. I get scareder.

It is dark now. It is dark and we are all alone at the park.

Davie looks scared too. We sit by each other on the spinny thing. But we don't spin. We don't spin. We don't spin.

I look at Davie a lot. I keep lookin' at him. He don't look at me, though. He is lookin' around. Like he is playin' hide and seek. And he is the looker.

It is dark still. I am cold and I see the stars. Davie is not okay. He keeps tellin' me, "Mommy is coming back," but I don't believe him. I am scared. I am scared. I am scared. I am scared. I want to go inside. I want to be in my bed. I want to go home and be with Mommy and FunnyBunny. I want my FunnyBunny. I want FunnyBunny.

I start to cry cuz I am scared real bad.

"Davie, I am scared. I am cold. I want to go home."

Davie puts his arm around me.

"It's okay. Mom's coming. We'll go home soon. Just a little while. Don't cry. It's okay."

I am still scared and crying. But Davie is being nice so I am kinda better.

NINE TO ELEVEN YEARS OLD
House on Bear Street

We sit in the dark, cold garage and I watch her smoke her minty cigarettes and drink her vodka in her pink cup.

I like being out here with her because she talks to me. She's my best friend. She likes talking to me out here. Out here when she smokes and drinks. No one else is here and I get to be all alone with her. I matter. She loves me. She needs me too.

She asks what she should do. She looks at me and doesn't know. She's scared. I can tell she's scared and she looks lost.

I can smell the vodka and minty cigarettes on her breath. Sometimes I wish that my breath would smell like that too. But I've tasted that stuff and it's disgusting. The smell makes me want to throw up.

She needs me. She needs me because I am her best friend and I'm smart and she loves me. She tells me all the time that I'm her best friend. It makes me feel special. She tells me all the time that I'm the only one she can talk to about "this stuff." Pretty much, that means Bill.

She trusts me. But she doesn't listen to me.

I sit in the dark next to her and I smell the smoke and the vodka and the mint and I tell her to leave him. "Just leave him, Mom."

Even when I just think about it and tell her to leave him I get the most excited, swirly, happy, hoping feeling in my body. Like something great is about to happen. I just wish she would do it already. I hate him. He's mean. He is mean and hurts us and I never know what is going to happen when he's around.

I tell her again. "Just leave him, Mom. You can do it. We'll be okay. Everything will be okay."

Again, I get the swirly, excited, happy, hoping feeling that I get when I do a flip on the trampoline.

She looks at me, scared. She looks at me scared and I know that she isn't going to do it.

She starts to talk about money and bills and the house and how she can't make it on her own and how she's afraid of him and this and that and this and that.

The swirly, excited, happy, hoping feeling goes away. The swirly feeling is gone.

Rage and fear and the sick, sick stomach feelings are back.

There is no hope.

EIGHTEEN YEARS OLD

I look over at him. I am so scared. I am so scared. I don't know if I can go through with this. I don't know if I can do this. I know they're going to be there and I don't know if I can face them.

I look over at him. He looks at me. He grabs my hand.

It's okay. Everything is going to be okay.

I look at him in silence. No, it's not. It is definitely not okay. This is not okay. This is SO NOT OKAY!! I don't know if I can do this. I don't know if I can go through with this. THIS FUCKING SUCKS!! Only whores do this. Only sluts do this. I am a fucking whore. A fucking slut.

As we turn into the alley, we see them everywhere. They are fucking everywhere. They know we're coming. They've been waiting for us. They know we're coming. They're waiting for us. Fuck. They're fucking everywhere.

"WHAT THE FUCK! SEAN, THEY TOLD US TO COME IN THE ALLEY! THEY TOLD US THEY WOULDN'T BE HERE!! THEY AREN'T SUPPOSED TO BE HERE!"

"Oh shit," Sean says.

My heart is racing. I'm terrified. I'm horrified. I can't do this. I can't fucking do this. They are everywhere. My stomach feels sick. I feel like I'm going to hurl. I feel like I almost got into a car accident. My heart won't stop racing. I'm sick. I'm sick. I'm so fucking sick.

As we near the parking lot they start to swarm around the car. They're all swarming us. They're a mob and they hate us. I see the hatred in their eyes. They're all looking at us like we are the scum of the earth. We are scum. We are scum. I am fucking scum. I can't do this. I am going to pass out. I'm getting dizzy. I'm seeing spots. Black-and-white spots.

"Arabella, we have to get out and we have to get in there, quick."

I look up. Sean has parked the car and they're fucking everywhere. They're swarming us. They're all around the car.

Tons of them. Women, men, young, old . . .

As I look out the window, I can feel the hatred from their eyes searing my heart. The hatred is burning holes through my skin. My fucking skin is burning. The hate is burning my skin. My skin is on fire. I'm on fire. BURN. FLAMES. HATRED. HATE. HATE. SCUM. HATE.

"Arabella!! We have to go!"

I look over at Sean. Behind him I see faces outside of the car. All I see is HATRED. I have never seen so many people look at me with that look. They want me dead. They want me to die. They want me dead. They want me to fucking die. To burn alive.

I wish I was dead. Fucking dead.

"Where are the other people? There were supposed to be people meeting us at the car. Where are they?"

"I don't know. We have to go. Okay Arabella? We have to go."

Tears stream down my face. A steady, salty stream streaks down my cheeks. I can't do this. I can't do this. I am evil. I am evil. I can't do this. I can't do this. I CANNOT do this.

Before I know what is happening, my door is open. Sean is there. But I don't see Sean.

I see SCREAMING. HATE. LOATHE. DISGUST. HATEFUL RAGE.

They want me dead.

They scream.

"MURDERER!"

"BABY KILLER!"

"YOU'RE GOING TO HELL!"

"YOU'RE GOING TO BURN IN HELL!"

"YOU'RE A SINNER AND A MURDERER AND YOU'RE GOING TO BURN IN HELL FOR ETERNITY!"

I feel as if I'm going to pass out. I look around. Someone has me by the arm and I am walking to the door. All around me the people who want me dead are waving huge signs in slow motion. They're all screaming hatred and waving signs with bloody, ripped-apart babies on them. There are huge pictures of bloody, ripped-apart babies on them. There are pictures of bloody, ripped-up babies on them and HATE words.

The baby's head is ripped open. THE BABY HAS ONLY HALF OF A HEAD. IT'S RIPPED IN HALF AND BLOODY! THE BABY IS COVERED IN BLOOD AND GUTS. BLOOD AND GUTS. BABY BLOOD. BABY GUTS. BLOOD. GUTS. BABY. BABY. BABY.

They scream louder as I get closer to the door.

"MURDERER!"

"BABY KILLER!"

"YOU'RE A MURDERER!"
"YOU'RE GOING STRAIGHT TO HELL!"
"YOU SHOULD BE IN PRISON! YOU MURDERER!"
"GOD IS GOING TO PUNISH YOU!"
"YOU'RE GOING TO SPEND ETERNITY IN DAMNATION!"
"YOU'RE A MURDERER!"
"YOU'RE A BABY KILLER!"

Sean grabs the door and as I walk in I hear one last voice clearly.

"MOMMY, PLEASE DON'T KILL ME!"

I turn to see who could make themselves sound so young.

Through my tears I see a tiny, red-haired girl around ten years old with a sign that's bigger than she is. It has a picture of a bloody, ripped-up baby on it.

She looks at me with a look I've never seen on a child. I've never seen a child look like her. Never. Ever. Never-ever.

Her eyes burn through my chest and HATE my heart. She HATES me. SHE HATES me. SHE HATES ME.

I HATE me!

SEVEN TO NINE YEARS OLD
House on Pine Road

I walk up our dirt road chewing on some sort of sticky, sweet candy. I look down and open the paper bag. Every color wrapper I can imagine. I got every kind of candy I could ever want. I got so much candy! I have gum and taffy and hard candy and Tootsie Rolls. I LOVE TOOTSIE ROLLS. They're my favorite. Chewy and soft and brown. There is not much left, though. I think I ate half of the bag on the walk home. Oh well. I still have half the bag left.

I look up into the driveway. Oh good. Mom is home. But so is Bill. I hate Bill. I mean, I hate my dad. He is not my real dad. I hate calling him Dad. He is not my real dad. Oh well, at least Mom is home and I got my candy.

I come in the garage door and walk through the basement. I wonder if the babysitter left yet. Mom is home, so she probably did.

I got so much candy. I grip the top of the bag. It is wrinkled and full of wrappers. I ate almost all of it on the way home. But I still have some left.

Candy. Candy. Candy. I love Candy. Candy makes me smile. Candy is so sweet. I can get it a lot and I can eat it and smile. It is so sweet. I Love Candy!

I hate this basement. It's dark and scary.

I'm gonna say hi to Mom and go into my room and eat the rest of the bag. There is not that much left. Only half the bag. So I am gonna go into my room and eat the rest of the bag full of sweet candy.

This is the only sweet stuff I ever get. Mom only has brown bread and corn flakes or Cheerios. We don't get to eat sweet stuff except when we go to Grandma's and except when I get to go to the store and get candy. They are one penny a piece for little pieces and three pennies for really big pieces. I get lots of one penny ones and less really big ones.

My babysitter is so nice. She let me and my friend go to the Quick Stop and get candy with the pennies we saved. I cannot remember her name but she is the daughter of my mom's mean boss. She is really old. I think she is in high school.

I walk through my mom and Bill's–I mean my dad's—room. Their room always smells funny. It smells like my mom's bad breath. It smells like bad breath in a box. And you open the box and the smell is all stinky inside. I don't like the way their room smells.

When I get upstairs, Mom, Bill, and my babysitter are sitting in the living room. They look mad.

"Hi, Mom."

"WHERE HAVE YOU BEEN?"

"I went to the Quick Stop. She said I could go."

I look at her so that she can tell them that she said I could go. Tell them, babysitter; you said I could go.

She lies.

"No, I didn't say she could go," she says. She looks at my mom and says, "I didn't know that she was there."

WHAT?!?!? LIAR!! She IS A LIAR!! Why is she lying? She said I could go. She said I could go. LIAR!! Her pants are on fire!

"Mom, she *did* say I could go!"

I look at the babysitter.

"I asked you if me and my friend could go to the Quick Stop and you said we could. You said we could. *You did!* Remember? Mom, she said I could go! I promise!"

My mom and Bill are getting madder. They look really mad. My mom looks at me and I can tell that she don't believe me.

She don't believe me and I am telling the truth. This happens all the time. She never believes me when I am telling the truth. I am telling the truth. I swear I am telling the truth.

"Arabella, why are you lying? What have I told you about lying? You need to tell the truth or you're going to be in a lot of trouble!"

I look at Bill. I know I'm going to get into a lot of trouble even though I am telling the truth.

"Mom, I am telling the truth! She told me I could go to the Quick Stop! I swear! I swear and hope to die!"

The babysitter speaks. Lies.

"No, I never told her that she could go to the store. She's lying."

Why is she doing this? Why is she saying that she don't know that I was there? She *did* know that I was there. I start to cry. No one believes me. No one ever believes me. I am telling the truth and no one ever believes me. She said I could go. I swear!

"Why are you crying? Because you know you're lying? Are you ready to tell the truth now?"

"I *am* telling you the truth. I swear I am telling you the truth. I swear. Mom, please believe me! She's lying."

"She has no reason to lie, Arabella. You go to your room and think about what you've done and when you're ready to tell the truth, you can come out."

I am bawling now. I am bawling hard, golf-ball-sized tears. Hard and betrayed. Hard and full of RAGE. As I walk to my room I feel the freak-out coming. I feel my tummy get tight and sick feeling. I feel my head start to throb. I feel the urge. The urge to break stuff. To throw stuff. To scream and throw my socks around. I want to tear all of the clothes out of my closet and bite them and rip them to pieces. I want them to believe me.

WHY DON'T THEY BELIEVE ME!! I AM TELLING THE TRUTH. I AM TELLING THE TRUTH AND THEY DON'T BELIEVE ME. I HATE THEM! I HATE THEM! I HATE THEM!

This isn't fair. This isn't FAIR! THIS ISN'T FAIR!! I want to run away. I want to run away because no one loves me or believes me. They all hate me and think that I am stupid. My mom loves Scooter more than me and Bill loves Rusty more than me. Why don't they believe me? Why don't they believe me? Why? Why? Why?

I feel the freaky, tummy meanness inside of me. I shut my bedroom door. I throw the brown paper bag across the room and I look at my bed.

I run over to it and tear off all of the blankets and throw them around the room. I throw my dolls on the floor. I grab everything I see and throw it. I am bawling. No one loves me. No one believes me. I'm telling the truth! I am sick to my stomach. Freak out. Freak out. FREAK OUT!

Scream. I need to scream. I need to scream. I need to scream. I can't scream. I can't cuz Bill and Mom will get me. I'll get into trouble. My head is pounding. Throbbing. My tears are pounding on my face. My tears beat my face. They punch my face and my head throbs.

Suddenly the door opens and Bill is standing there. He is as tall as the door and I hate him. I am small and scared and shrinking. I want to hide under the bed. He is mad. He says to come with him. He has a belt in his hand.

"No," I cry. "No, I did not do it. I did not lie. She said I could . . ."

He grabs me by the arm and yanks me off the bed. He drags me down to the bad breath box. He is taking me to the bad breath box. He is mad and he is taking me to the bad breath box with a belt in his hand.

The curtains are shut. It is not as light as it was when I came home. It is dark. He looks at me and says that I lied and now I have to face my punishment.

I cry. I cry. My head throbs. My tears are punching my face. No. Please, Dad. Please.

He sits on the chair. He has a big leather belt in his hand. He has a big leather belt and he is mad.

"Pull your pants down."

"No, I do not want to," I cry.

"PULL YOUR PANTS DOWN NOW!"

I stand there crying. I stand there crying and shrinking and tears are punching me in the face. Scared. Scared. Scared.

"ARABELLA! PULL YOUR PANTS DOWN RIGHT NOW OR I'LL DO IT FOR YOU!"

I stand there crying. I am so scared. He is going to see my undies. He is going to see me in my undies. I do not want my dad to see me in my undies.

Shame. Shame. Shame. Shame. Shame.

I cry and I pull my pants down.

"YOUR UNDERWEAR TOO!"

I look at him through the tears that won't stop beating on my face. He is serious and I am scared. I have to do what he says.

Humiliation. Humiliated. Degraded. Dishonored. Shamed. Shamed. Shame.

I pull my undies off and stand in the dark, smelly, bad breath box. I am in a box and my tears will not stop beating down my cheeks.

He is mad. He is still mad. He reaches over and grabs my arm and lays me over his lap.

WHACK!

WHACK!

WHACK WHACK WHACK WHACK!

I cry out in pain.

My bottom stings. It hurts so bad and he can see my bottom and my down there. I cry and sting and cry and sting.

WHACK!

WHACK!

WHACK!

He hits me as hard as his arm can hit me. My bottom feels like someone has cut it up and poured stingy stuff on it. I cry and shame. Cry and shame.

WHACK!

WHACK!

I disappear. I disappear into the cuts and stingy stuff and pain and shame and the tears punching me. I disappear into the smelly bad breath box. I disappear . . . WHACK . . . whack . . . whack . . . whack . . . whack . . . whack . . . whack . . . whack . . .

THREE TO FIVE YEARS OLD

Me and Davie are chasing each other around the room.

We run around the couch that our real daddy is sitting on. A crowd is cheering and people in costumes are throwing a ball. They are playing a game. My real daddy is watching them play a game on TV.

My real daddy is big like Bill. He is as tall as a door too. He has a shiny head on top, though. But he has black hair on the sides by his ears. He is my real daddy. He is big and I never get to see him. This is so fun.

"You two calm down; I'm trying to watch the game."

Me and Davie are having fun chasing each other around the couch. I am screaming a fun scream. Not a scary one. Davie is trying to get me. He wants to hold me down and tickle me. I giggle and smile and play with Davie.

"I SAID YOU TWO CALM DOWN! STOP CHASING EACH OTHER AROUND THE HOUSE! I'M TRYING TO WATCH THE GAME!"

We are having fun. We are chasing each other and Davie wants to get me so he can hold me down and tickle me. He wants to hold me down and tickle me. We are having fun. And my real daddy is watching a game.

I am running around the couch and he is trying to get me.

RIP!

My real daddy grabs me by my hair. It hurts so bad!! My hair is going to pull out of my head. My head is going to rip off.

I scream, "OWIE! OWIE! OWIE!"

It hurts, it hurts, it hurts my head real bad. My hair is going to rip right off. My head hurts. I am crying. I am crying in pain cuz my head is going to rip off of my body.

"I SAID YOU TWO CALM DOWN! SINCE YOU BRATS CAN'T LISTEN, YOU'RE GOING OUTSIDE FOR THE REST OF THE GAME!"

My real daddy shoves us outside the front door.

I cry. Davie cries. We sit outside the door. I cry and my head hurts. My hair stings. My hair stings cuz my real daddy grabbed me and threw me outside by my hair.

It is getting darker. Me and Davie have been sitting here forever. For like ten bazillion hours. My hair still hurts and my real daddy is mad at us.

My real daddy lives in a big building. It is tall. He lives in a building with lots of other people. We sit on the ground by his door up high and people walk past us. We all share the place outside of my real daddy's door. People walk past and I think that my head is starting to hurt less.

My real daddy is mad at me and my hair hurts less now. I'm a bad girl. Davie is a bad boy too. We did not listen to my real daddy when he said not to run around. We are bad and we are in big trouble. That is why he ripped our hair out. He ripped our hair out because we are really bad. I'm a bad girl and Davie is a bad boy. We are bad and our real daddy is mad at us.

It is getting darker.

TWENTY-THREE YEARS OLD

I wake up again, my head throbbing, pounding, and I need water. I need water again. Every morning it's the same. My head throbs.

I got ran over again last night. Throbbing. Pounding. A constant dead thud. Thud. Thud. Thud. My head is a constant dead thud.

I roll over and stretch and feel my nakedness. OH FUCK! Not again. What did I do last night? Who did I fuck?

FUCK! FUCK! FUCK!

My head throbs and thuds and pulses in pain. My mouth is full of cotton. Cotton that tastes like it was soaked in cigarette butts and warm, cheap beer. I need water. I have to get up and get water. I need wetness in my mouth and down my throat. I need to swallow the cotton balls.

I lie here and tell myself to get up. My eyes—thick, puffy, red, heavy—are swollen. It's a workout opening them. It's like lifting weights. I'm pumping iron to open my eyes. I have barbells hanging from my top eyelashes.

I groan. I groan. Groan. Lift my eyes. I need water and I need to lift my eyes. What happened last night? This has to stop. Every night it's the same. I'm a fucking slut. I know that I must have fucked someone because I am naked. I'm naked and I was drunk. So, I fucked. I just don't know who.

Think. I have to think. I can't think. My head is too swollen. My eyes are too swollen. The cotton balls are too swollen. I have to think. Who did I fuck? Who was it this time? Think. Scan. Scan. Remember, Bella. Remember, Bella. What happened? Remember, Bella.

FLASH!

Sitting in my living room in front of the fireplace. I'm dressed up in my sexiest, shortest skirt and top. I have on my come-fuck-me boots. My hooker boots. That's what my friend calls them. Hooker boots. They're sexy. I look fucking hot in them. Every guy wants me when I put on this outfit. My short skirt and booby-top and hooker boots. I'm a babe. And guys want me. They want me because I am hot. I am hot. I am hot, hot, hot . . .

I am so hot. I feel like I'm in an oven. Sweat beads on my forehead. My head throbs and pounds and I'm in an oven. The beer-soaked, cigarette-butt-flavored cotton balls are growing and I'm burning in a fire. I need to throw up. God, I have to throw up. Oh fuck. I'm going to throw up.

I run to the toilet, if you can call this running. My body is heavy. There are weights on my eyes and my arms and my head and my legs and my toes. I am dead. My body is dying. I am heavy and I am dying.

I hit the toilet and my stomach flexes. It pushes and flexes and nothing comes out. I hang onto the edge and flex and push and spit. Spit and flex and push.

FLASH!

I'm sitting in the living room in my sexy outfit with two men. They're both firemen. They're both hot. One is tall with reddish hair and the other is a tall brunette. They're hot and I'm hot. They want me. I want them. I've drunk enough to know that they're the two who will do it tonight. They will do it. They will do it because they want me. Want me. They want me . . .

I heave and flex and spit and nothing comes out. I stare at the water, my face inches from the top. My head has a weight on it and the weight pushes my head closer and closer to the water.

FLASH!

I am naked on my bed. I am naked and the light, the ceiling light, is on. The bright one. Not the lamps. I am on the bed naked on my hands and knees . . .

UUUUHHHHH! I have to puke. Tears well in my eyes as my stomach flexes and contracts. It contracts and tightens and screams at me. I'm being punished because I am a BIG, fucking slut. I'm a slut and I'm a drunk and I'm a whore.

I plead. Oh my God. Please, let me die. Let me die. Let me throw up. Please let me throw the fuck up and I'll feel better. I'll feel better and my stomach will stop flexing and contracting and raging at me. Punishing me. Hating me. Destroying me.

FLASH!

I'm on my hands and knees. I'm doggy-style, naked, and these hot men have no shirts on. They have no shirts on and they are fucking hot. They are firemen. Two firemen and they want me. They want me. They want to fuck me because I am hot. Two of them. Two firemen! . . .

I don't know how they got into the house. They must have come in with me, but I don't remember where I met them. I can't remember where I met them. Think. Think, Bella. Think.

BLANK ... ... BLANK ... ... BLANK ... ... BLANK ... ... BLANK ... ...

I can't remember where I met them. I can't remember this because I can't remember a lot. When I drink, I can't remember how I get home sometimes. I get home and wake up and feel run over. I look outside to make sure that I didn't get run over and find my truck safe in the driveway. No scratches and no dents. I get home but I don't remember how.

FLASH!

I'm doggy-style and the light is bright and these two firemen with bulging pecs and six-pack abs are shirtless and wearing underwear. Both of their cocks are hard. Their cocks are hard through their underwear. One fireman is in boxers and one is in boxer-briefs. They look like Calvin Klein underwear models. They are hard and hot and firemen. They look at me with desire. They

want me and think I'm hot. They want to fuck me. Because I am
hot . . .

I want to die. The throbbing has spread to my arms and legs
and ears and nose. My whole body is throbbing and aching and
pounding and thirsty. Flexing. Stomach flexing and heaving and
I grip the toilet and heave dry. Spit and dry. Dry heaves. Cotton
contracting. Cotton like butts and beer and acid. Stomach acid
soaks into the cotton. I want to die. Please let me die. I'm a
fucking drunk and slut and I want to die. I need to die. Die now.

   FLASH!
   I'm doggy-style and one hot fireman is behind me. His cock
is in me. He is fucking me. In and out. In and out. I am hot. He
wants me. Wants me. Me. The other is in my mouth. His cock is
huge and it's in my mouth. I am being pushed from behind by
the other fireman's cock. And there's one in my mouth. They're
loving it. I am doing what I am supposed to be doing because they
want me . . .

   FLASH!
   I hate giving head. His cock is too big. I hate it, but I do it
because they want me and that's all that matters. They want me.
I need want. I need them to want me. They want me and I don't
care that I hate giving head. I'm used to it . . .

I grip the toilet and suck on the cotton balls full of acid. They
are full of acid and I think. I remember and think. I groan. I hate
giving head.

   FLASH!
   I'm five or six years old and I'm giving head. I am giving head
because I am a cousin-fucking whore . . .

I release the toilet and the contracting and flexing subsides. The acid-butt-beer-flavored cotton balls are still in my mouth. I need water. I need to drink. I need to drink water. I need to drink and smoke and not feel this. I need pot. Weed will take away the pain. Weed will take away the pain and I will feel sleep. I will sleep and I will no longer not feel.

The acidy, cheap, cigarette-butt-and warm beer-flavored, cotton balls will disappear in my sleep.

The flexing will disappear.

The contracting will disappear.

The weights will disappear.

The cousin-fucking will disappear.

The shame will disappear.

The whore will disappear.

The FLASHES will disappear.

And I will disappear.

SEVEN TO TEN YEARS OLD

All the adults are upstairs. All of us kids are downstairs. We are at my grandma and grandpa's house. We're downstairs playing bar. We play bar a lot. My grandma has a bar downstairs and we take turns being bartenders.

The adults are upstairs playing bar too. They have cocktails, so we go downstairs and play bar like them. We act like we drink. Matt and Dave are pouring us drinks. We use Mountain Dew, Pepsi, Dr. Pepper, 7Up, orange and grape soda, Coke, and Pepsi. I like the orange and the Mountain Dew. They are the best.

On the walls behind the bar there are little porcelain women wearing little swimsuits like the ones from the time when my grandma was really young. They have bottoms that look like shorts and tops that look like bras. The women are all perfect and pretty. I wish I looked like them. Matt and Dave talk about them and how they think that they are hot. They want girls that look just like the porcelain women.

Matt asks me what kind of drink I want. He calls me miss and treats me like a customer. He is flirty with me. He treats me like one of the porcelain women.

He looks at me like boys at school look at me who like me. He looks at me like he wants to be my boyfriend. He looks at me like I'm special. I am special to him.

He thinks I'm special. He winks at me. Matt winks at *me*. He is cute. He thinks I'm cute. He looks at me like I'm one of the porcelain women in the old-timey swimsuits. He likes me and I like it.

I feel bad at the same time. I feel bad in my stomach sometimes. I feel bad because I cannot tell anyone. I know that what I can't tell about is bad because he tells me not to tell anyone when he does stuff that is physical. That is what he calls it. Physical. He sings, "Let's get physical. Let me hear your body talk." And he points at me when he sings it.

Sometimes he says stuff like, "Incest is best; put your cousin to the test." He looks at me and he smiles when he says it. But he never says it when the parents are around. He looks at me and he gives me that look that he gives me before we get physical. Cuz he thinks I'm special and he likes to do stuff to me. I'm not sure what incest is. But I know I cannot say it in front of the adults. And I know that it means getting physical.

That makes me feel weird, but he thinks I'm special and I like being around him because he never hurts me. He never makes fun of me and he never hits me. Dave does that and I do not like it. Bill does too. My mom does too. So that's why I like to be here with Matt. He makes me feel good even though sometimes it feels bad in my stomach.

Sometimes Matt comes over to Grandma's just to see me. And he likes it when I spend the night at his house. And he likes to spend the night here at Grandma's. He thinks I'm special and he likes to be around me. He thinks I'm nice.

Now me and Jessica play bartenders. We pour Matt and Dave drinks. We are not flirty and we do not wink. But we call them sir and mister.

Our littlest cousin is upstairs with the adults. She's too young to be downstairs with us because we play bar and Atari.

Matt is the same age as my brother Dave. He is two grades higher than me. Jessica is one grade higher than me. I'm the youngest except for Katie. She is a few years younger than me. I used to be the youngest but not anymore.

We are done with our drinks and we go over to the couch. It's an old-timey couch. It has funny colors like the rest of the house. Matt turns the lights off. I can hear Dave and Jessica on the other couch. They are doing stuff too.

Matt gets on top of me and he kisses me. He uses his tongue like usual. His lips are dry and crackly. Like usual. They are chapped like my lips are in the winter in the snow and cold. He kisses me and he pushes his body on me. It feels good. But it feels bad in my stomach.

It feels good between my legs. Him pushing his body on me feels good between my legs. But it also feels bad because I know that I am not supposed to be doing it. Even though we are not blood-related, Matt told me never to tell anyone and I know that I cannot because it's bad. Boys are not supposed to touch me down there. That is bad.

I do not know what Dave and Jessica are doing but I hear them making noises too. Sometimes they do physical stuff too. But never like Matt does to me. Matt likes me more than Dave likes Jessica. Jessica is really fat.

Matt likes to get dirty and pull my pants off and touch me and lick me in my privates. He does it a lot. He likes me to touch him and suck on his privates. I do that a lot. He likes to put his privates in my privates. He thinks I'm special. He likes me and thinks I'm pretty too. Even though I'm younger than him, he thinks I'm pretty.

He thinks I'm special and he likes me more than Dave likes Jessica because I look like one of the porcelain women. Except I do not have boobs. I do not have boobs cuz I'm too young to.

But he told me I looked like the porcelain woman in the yellow old-timey suit. She has brown hair and blue eyes like me. He thinks I look like her and he thinks she's pretty. He thinks I'm special so I do the physical stuff with him because he thinks that. I do it because it feels good and no one else makes me feel good like he does. He loves me.

My aunt calls.

"WHY ARE THE LIGHTS OFF DOWN THERE?"

Matt rips his hands out from my pants and jumps up and zips his pants.

"WE'RE PLAYING HIDE AND GO SEEK IN THE DARK, MOM," Matt shouts back.

"I DON'T CARE; TURN THE LIGHTS BACK ON!"

Matt turns the lights on.

We all look around at each other and feel funny.

Dave gets up to play Atari.

Jessica decides to go upstairs.

Matt winks at me and whispers that we will get physical later. I believe him because he means what he says. He is not like my mom. When he says he will do stuff, he will. I cannot wait. Even if it is bad. I am excited to see him later.

He makes me feel good. He thinks I'm special. He is the only one who thinks I'm special. I'm special to him.

I'm pretty like the porcelain woman.

SEVENTEEN YEARS OLD

"We have to stop and get money."

"Okay," Lacey tells me. She's driving.

I'm in the front seat, and Nicki and Ellie are in the back.

We're going to Great Falls to go dancing at the club we like to dance at. It's an all-ages club.

I'm wearing my Lady-in-Red dress. It's ankle length, with a slit up to my thigh. It has thick straps and a V-neck. It's form fitting, and I feel really pretty in it. Of course, I don't look like my friends. They're all so much prettier than me. But I feel prettier than usual in this dress.

I look over at Lacey and smile. She's wearing her forest green dress. It's the exact same style as mine except that she has boobs that fill in the top. She has big boobs. I am so BIG, but I have no boobs. I've always wondered why my mom has such big, perfect, perky boobs and I have none. I barely fill an A-cup. Any time I buy a dress the top is always too big. My thighs are fat. My butt is fat and my hips are fat. Getting a dress to fit my fat bottom half almost always guarantees that the top will bag because I'm as flat as a wall.

I hate my body. I really hate it. Guys don't want someone who has no boobs. They want women with big ones. I don't understand what happened to me. I ask my mom this a lot. Why am I flat? I hate my boobs.

She tells me that I have a body just like my aunt. My aunt is like ten feet tall and flat as a wall. It's not a compliment. My mom never makes me feel good about my body.

I look at Lacey's legs. They are perfectly thin. Perfect. Fucking perfect.

We share clothes. Jeans, tops, and shoes. Not bras, though. But no one would think we could by looking at us.

Her legs are long and thin. Mine are muscular and thick. I hate them. I really fucking hate them. My mom tells me that I have the same body she has. Except for the fact that I have no boobs and I am way BIGger. I'm five foot nine and she's five foot pretty-much-nothing.

Bill used to tell her that she has thunder thighs and football player thighs. Then she would tell me that I had the same thighs as her. I hate my fucking thighs. I have football player thighs. I'm a fucking fat football player with no boobs. I'm so flat that my chest indents. I hate my fucking body. But I look prettier in this dress than I do in regular clothes.

I look down at Lacey's legs. She doesn't have thunder thighs. All I can think is that she doesn't have thunder thighs and I do. She has stick legs and I have thunder thighs. I have thunder thighs

I have thunder thighs I have thunder thighs. Guys want sticks.
They don't want thunder thighs.

All I can think is that I wish I had her body. I wish I had her
legs and her boobs and then guys would want me like they do her.
I want to have the guys want me like they do her. I would give
anything to have the guys want me like they do her.

All I've ever wanted was to be thin like Lacey. She's so lucky.
She has thin thighs and big boobs. I wish I had her body. I wish
I had her body. I hate my body. I am fat and flat. Fat and flat.
Fucking Fat and Flat!

I would give my right arm to be thin and have big boobs.
That's all I've ever wanted; I know that then I would be so happy.

Nicki's in the back seat. She borrowed my little blue velvet
dress. It fits her much better than it does me. She has boobs and
is tiny and blonde. She's like a shorter version of a Barbie doll. I
look like a fucking blimp in that dress compared to her. A fucking
blimp! A blimp with thunder thighs.

She has the same build as my mom except she's thinner than
my mom.

But she doesn't eat. She thinks she's fat, but she has a perfect
body. She has a perfect fucking body.

I think she's fucking stupid to think that she's fat. How she
can possibly look in the mirror and think she's fat is beyond my
comprehension. Sometimes I think she does it for attention. She
just wants people to tell her, "No, you're not fat." I hate when
skinny girls think they're fat. It really pisses me off.

I would kill to have her body. Guys always want Nicki because
she has the perfect body. I wish I had a perfect body and then I
would be happy because guys would want me.

Ellie's sitting next to Nicki. I look back to see her. She's
gorgeous. She's gorgeous and she thinks she's ugly and too
skinny. She's fucking crazy. She hates her body as much as
I hate mine. But she's fucking crazy. At least she isn't fat.

She's skinny and pretty and has nothing to worry about. She doesn't understand what it's like to be so fat. Skinny girls never understand.

She *is* skinny. Actually, she's *really* skinny. But models are skinny. She could be a model. She looks just like a young Winona Ryder. She could be a model, and next to her I look like a fucking house.

I look at her boobs. They're the same size as mine, but she weighs at least thirty pounds less than me. She weighs less than me so she looks good with smaller boobs. She looks like a runway model. I'm just a BIG fucking fat cow with small boobs.

We pull up to my mom's work. I have to get my allowance.

We decide to all go inside and show off our outfits.

We all walk inside the office feeling like we look great.

You can tell by the way we're walking. We got the swagger, baby.

My mom is finishing a woman's makeup.

"Hi, Mom. I need my allowance."

"Did you clean the house?" she asks without looking at us.

"Yeah, it's done. We're in a hurry."

"Look in my purse."

As I look in her purse for my ten bucks the girls all say hi to her.

I get the ten bucks. We all stand by her station and show off our dresses.

Then she sees us.

"Wow! Look at you girls!"

She walks up to Nicki who's wearing my blue dress and has the same body as my mom. She speaks again.

"Isn't this your dress, Arabella?"

"Yeah, it's mine."

"It looks so different on *you*, Nicki."

"Thanks," Nicki says. She's a little uncomfortable with my mom's arm around her.

My mom speaks again.

"Well, I can tell who has the best body out of all of you!"

She looks Nicki up and down then looks herself up and down and raises her eyebrows and laughs her loud, annoying laugh. Loud. Obnoxious. Annoying. RAGE!

SMACK! SMACK! SMACK! SMACK!

One smack for each of us.

I want to fucking die. I want to FUCKING DIE. I WANT TO FUCKING DIE!

I look around at my friends. They have no smiles left on their faces. They feel like shit. For that minute they feel what I have felt for the past seventeen years of my life. They feel like they are less than. They feel ugly and they feel worthless. Valueless. Hurt. Fucking hurt.

They've just experienced a tiny bit of what I experience every day with my mother. Every day it's a fucking competition. Every day it's about her body and my body. Every day I lose. Every day I lose because I am BIG and I don't look like her.

I am BIG and fat and I am a loser.

I am flat as a board and I am a loser.

I have a body just like my Amazon aunt and I am a loser.

I feel rage. Fucking Rage. FUCKING RAGE! I want to punch my fucking idiot of a mother in the face and tell her to go fuck herself. I fucking hate her.

I look at my joyless friends.

I look at her.

RAGE. FUCKING RAGE. I WANT TO SMACK HER. POUND HER. TEAR ALL OF HER HAIR OUT.

But I don't.

I say, "Thanks a lot mom. Let's go, you guys."

We leave and I am full of Rage. RAGE. I am embarrassed. RAGE and EMBARRASSMENT. RAGE and EMBARRASSMENT.

I tell my friends how fucking sorry I am. I am so sorry. I am so sorry. I am so sorry. *I am so fucking sorry!* I say, "It's not true. My mom is fucked up and I hate her. I am so sorry that she said that to you."

They tell me it's not my fault and they mean it. But they're affected. They're affected like I've been affected my whole life. They feel in this moment what I have felt my whole life. I fucking hate her for that. I fucking hate her, period. I just hate her.

I want to smash in my mom's face for making them feel like she makes me feel. I hate her and I wish I could take back her stupid, fucking idiotic comment.

They're affected. I'm affected. We're all affected.

So we smoke a bowl and sing to music the whole way to Great Falls.

For the effect.

SEVEN TO NINE YEARS OLD

House on Pine Road

I stare at my plate. I have been staring at it for a bazillion years.

All that is left is a pile of canned mushrooms. A pile of gross, slimy, canned mushrooms the size of a house. And a little bit of cream of mushroom soup from inside the casserole.

No one is at the table with me. I am alone. I have been staring at the plate for a hundred bazillion years while Bill watches TV.

Bill is in the next room. I don't look up at him or I will get in trouble. I have to look at my plate.

I have to stay here and finish my mushrooms. My nasty, slimy, stinky mushrooms. I hate mushrooms. I especially hate canned mushrooms. They make me gag. I want to puke when I smell them. I want to puke and barf because they are so gross. Slimy, brown, and gross.

I hate them and Bill makes me eat them. He makes me eat them and gets really mad when I don't. I hate Bill but I have to do what he says or he hits me.

I stare at the plate. I have to eat the mushrooms or I can't leave the table.

I take my fork and scoop some of the brown slime onto it. I put it in my mouth and hold my breath. I hold my breath cuz then I don't taste the stinkyness as much. I can still taste it but not as much.

I swallow and start to gag. I am gonna puke. I am gonna puke from the brown slime.

"OH GOD! DON'T BE SUCH A GODDAMN BABY AND EAT THE MUSHROOMS. YOU'RE STAYING AT THE TABLE UNTIL YOU EAT THEM. I DON'T CARE IF IT TAKES ALL FUCKING NIGHT!"

I beg him. "I can't eat them. I am gonna puke, Dad."

"STOP BEING SUCH A BRAT AND EAT THE GODDAMN MUSHROOMS!"

I start to get tears in my eyes. I am gonna throw up if I eat them. I look at the plate and the pile looks bigger than it did before I took my last bite. I cannot eat these. I am scared to cry. But I cannot help it. I am all alone at the table and Bill is making me eat the big pile of slime.

"STOP YOUR CRYING YOU CRY BABY AND EAT THE GOD-DAMN MUSHROOMS, OR I'LL COME OVER THERE AND SHOVE THEM DOWN YOUR FUCKING THROAT!"

I cry more as I scoop more of the slimy, brown, canned grossness on my fork. I cannot see through my tears where my mom is. I do not know where she is, but I know she is in the house. She is always in the house when bad things happen but she never does anything. She doesn't love me. She hates me. She loves Bill and I hate Bill. He is mean to me. He is mean to me and he makes fun of me. He makes fun of me and I get in trouble since he has been here.

I stick the fork in my mouth and hold my breath. I start to gag as I swallow. I cry and gag and cry and gag.

My stomach feels sick. My mouth starts to water. Oh no. My mouth is getting wet. WET! I'm gonna puke. I'm gonna puke. I'm gonna—

PUKE!

All over my plate.

I cry more. I am scared. Bill is going to come hit me; I know it. I am not allowed to cry and puke and be a baby. I cry more. Everything looks funny through my tears. It is all blurry. I am alone and everything is blurry and I smell puke.

"GODDAMN IT, ARABELLA!"

Oh no! He is gonna come hit me. I am really bad for throwing up. I wish I could hide. I wish I could hide. I wish I could hide. HIDE. HIDE. HIDE.

He stays on the couch. I do not understand. I stare at the plate and the smell of puke is making me gag more. The smell of puke is making my mouth wet again.

I cry and breathe through my mouth and wait for him to come hit me.

"NOW YOU GET TO SIT AT THE TABLE AND EAT EVERY-THING ON YOUR GODDAMN PLATE!"

I start to bawl. I cannot eat the puke. I cannot eat the puke. I am gonna throw up more if I smell it. I can smell the stinky puke. I look down and there are chunks of chewed, canned mushrooms in runny yellow juice. There is bubbly foam on it.

I cry.

"STOP CRYING YOU CRY BABY OR I'LL COME OVER THERE AND GIVE YOU SOMETHING TO CRY ABOUT!"

I cannot help it. I cry. The tears stream down my face and land on top of the foamy puke. They will not stop falling onto the puke. They keep falling and falling and making the pile of puke and chewed mushrooms bigger and bigger.

I'm all alone. I cry and wish Rusty was here. I wish that I was at my grandma's. I wish that I was at Karen's. I wish that I was out playing in the snow. I wish that I was petting Scooter and Joker.

I wish that my mom would come save me.

TWENTY-SIX YEARS OLD

Urgency.

Necessity.

Must have. Must have. Must have.

As I drive I picture it. I'll get there and run downstairs and sit on the couch and be there. There. Me and it. That's all there will be.

No phone. Shades drawn so that the neighbors can't see me. I have to be alone. I have to be alone and sink into the taste. I can taste it. I can feel it. I am there.

I pull into the driveway and I walk quickly around my car. I open the passenger door and grab the bags. There are four. Each filled with items from different places.

I can't get it all at one place because then people would know. They would know and I would be exposed. They would think I'm the disgusting person that I am.

As I open the door, I can taste it already. I can taste the sweetness melting in my mouth. I can taste the cold and the crunch and the sweetness of it.

It's all that matters. I don't care if my life ever starts, because it'll all be better after I'm on the couch. Anyway, it's not like it's drugs.

I need to lose weight but I don't care. All I care about is this. Nothing else. The world could disappear for all I care. I just want to have this, in my dark basement, by myself. Alone. By myself and I don't care about anything or anyone else. I have everything that I need.

I'm not hurting anyone and it's better than drugs. I used to be a drug addict and this is better than drugs. Anything is better than the way it was before. This is better than before. I am better than before.

I head straight downstairs. I don't put anything from the four bags away. I want all of it now. I need all of it now. I have to have all of it now. Have to have. Need. Want. Need. Urgency. Now.

I grab the remote and flip on the TV. It doesn't matter what's on. I don't care what's on. I don't care at all.

All I care about is getting it now. The TV is just filler. Just another way to distract myself from myself.

I tear open the first bag. I am a ravenous animal searching for my next hit. My next fix. I don't care where I get it, only that I have to have to have it now. Have to have it now. I must feel it on my tongue. Sweet. Cold. Rich. Cool. Crunchy. Sweet.

Now. Now. Now. Now. Now. Now. Now.

I take out the two in that bag. I set them on the TV dinner stand and I grab the next bag.

I take out the two from that bag and set them on the dinner stand. I grab the next bag.

I take out the three packages and set them on the stand. I grab the last bag.

I take the other three containers out and set them on the other dinner stand.

I open the three containers and the two pints from the first bag.

I grab the fork and dig into the first container. It melts in my mouth. I take another bite. Another bite. Another bite. Another bite. It's so sweet and creamy and smooth in my mouth. Another bite. Another bite. Another bite.

It melts on my tongue. The sweetest, most decadent, creamy, espresso-flavored cheesecake at the store. I eat. I eat. I eat. It's big. It's huge. It's mine.

I rip open one of the packages. There are six inside. I stuff one in my mouth. I chew. I stuff another and another and another. The white powder makes me thirsty.

I need wetness to wash this down. I could get up and get water.

I grab a pint and open it and dig into the cold wetness. It slides down my throat. The cold and sweet wetness slides down my throat. It washes the powder away and now I have a taste of it and I don't want to stop.

I bite another another another another. I'm an animal. An addict. A junkie. I have to have it now. All of it. I have to have all of it right now. Nothing else matters.

Bite. Another. Another. Another.

I see the frost on the others melting. I take their tops off and dig my spoon into each one. I alternate between the two.

I taste it all. All that matters is the taste, nothing else. The taste of sweetness. Carmel waffle cones and vanilla and chocolate and brownies and raspberry syrup and espresso-covered peanuts and Bailey's cream cheese and graham cracker and coconut and fruit-flavored cheese and cherries and chocolate flakes and sweet, sugary, powder-sweetened flour and taste and taste and taste.

I finish a pint and a cheesecake and a package of doughnuts. I move on to the next of each. There are two more packages of doughnuts. Two more pints and two more cheesecakes.

I eat. I bite. I taste. I have to have it. I fill. I am filling. I am slowly filling.

Filling it all. Filling it up. Filling it now.

Feeling less. Less. And less.

I finish another package of doughnuts and cheesecake.

I feel my stomach swelling and I don't care. I have a lot more to go. I can't stop now. I have to have it all now. All of it now.

If I could take it all in one big bite and hold it in my mouth and taste it forever, that bite wouldn't be big enough and forever wouldn't be long enough.

There's not enough. There's never enough. There is never enough. Never. Never. Never.

I grab another pint and alternate bites with the last cheesecake. Another package. I inhale, chew occasionally, but I taste.

All that matters is taste. No thoughts can penetrate. I think only of the flavors. The sweetness. The textures. The crunch. The smooth. The chewy. The cold. The warm. The dry. The coarse. The tart and the taste. The flavor. The taste. The fullness.

Nothing exists now. Absolutely nothing. Everything disappears. Everything is gone, everything good and everything bad. All that matters is what

I taste. What I feel in my mouth in this moment. Everything else does not exist.

I look down and there are packages. Only packages and a fat, disgusting stomach. It's over. It's gone and nothing is left.

The taste is gone. The cold is gone and only packages remain. There is no more left to fill myself. No more filling. I can't fill and so . . . it begins.

The drowsy, drugged self-condemnation. The gluttonous self-hatred. The shame. The loathing. Disgust. Rage. Hatred. Hatred. Hatred. Rage. RAGE. RAGE.

Drugged and drowsy Rage. Sleepy rage. Lethargic disgust.

But hate is strong. It perseveres. It penetrates. It is resilient and hardy.

It won't go anywhere. It's here to stay. With a vengeance.

You are fucking disgusting! You are a fucking pig! A fat, fucking pig! You are fucking disgusting! Look at the fat on your thighs! You are fucked up and no one wants you!

It continues.

It's no wonder that your mother doesn't love you. You're disgusting. No wonder you don't have a man. You are a gluttonous, fucking pig. No wonder you're all alone. You're a FUCKING PIG! A FAT, FUCKING PIG! You are fucking disgusting!

I look down at my thighs and scream at myself, a hateful wail.

I FUCKING HATE MYSELF! GODDDDDDDDDDDDDDDD!!!!!!!!

I look at my stomach. It is sticking out of my shirt and I want to cut it off. I want to take a razor and cut the fucking fat off of my stomach. I want to cut it, slice it. Hurt it. Kill it. Hate. RAGE. RAGE. RAGE.

The RAGE is in full force and my fat is the target.

I clench my teeth and start to cry.

I hate myself. I hate myself. I hate myself.

Nothing else exists.

NINE TO TWELVE YEARS OLD
House on Bear Street

Panic. Flight. Run. Move legs. Move legs. MOVE LEGS. MOVE LEGS!!

I have to run and get away and hide and find . . . door with . . . lock. Find door with lock. Find door with lock.

I run. I run into the only room in the house with a lock.

I run for my life into the bathroom and slam the door and just as I lock it the handle starts to turn back and forth. The door handle twists.

I stare at the lock to make sure that I shut it. Panic. Panic. Heart pounding. Pound. Pound. Pound. Pound. Fear. Terror. Terror. Terror.

Through the door I hear the demonic whispers.

"Die, Die, Die, Die, Die, Die, Die, Die . . . Kill, Kill, Kill, Kill, Kill, Kill, Kill, Kill.

"Die, Die, Die, Die, Die, Die, Die, Die . . . Kill, Kill, Kill, Kill, Kill, Kill, Kill, Kill.

"Die, Die, Die, Die, Die, Die, Die, Die . . . Kill, Kill, Kill, Kill, Kill, Kill, Kill, Kill.

"I'm gonna get yooooooooooou . . . I know yooooooooooou're iiiiiiiiiiiii-innn theeeeeeere . . ."

Heavy whispering. Breathing. Demonic whispers.

"Aaaaarrraaabbbeeellllaaaaaaaaaa, I'm going to get yooooooooooou."

I'm scared. I'm scared. I'm scared. I'm scared. He's going to kill me. He's going to kill me. He's going to kill me.

I breathe short, quick gasps of terror. I can't breathe. All I feel is panic. To survive. Fear. Panic. Panic. Panic. Terror.

I breathe in terror. Inhale terror and exhale terror. Short, fast breath of death. Breath of fear and breath of desperation. That's all I know.

As I breathe in horror, I look down at my feet. They're right in front of the crack of the door. OH GOD!

Panic. Panic. Panic. He can see my feet. He can slice my feet with the butcher knife. He can slice my feet.

Must move. Must move legs. Must move legs NOW!

I jump up onto the toilet and hold my breath.

I stand and don't move a muscle. I am a statue with a heart pounding through my stone chest. Cracking it. My heart is deafening. Oh God. My heart. My heart. My heart. He's gonna hear my heart. He's gonna hear my heart and he's gonna come cut it out. He's gonna kill me because he can hear my heart.

I try to hold my breath thinking that if I do then he won't hear my heart. He won't hear it and come in and kill me. He'll leave me alone. He'll leave me alone. Alone. I want to be alone. Alone. I wish I was alone.

Under the crack of the door I hear his hissssssing, terrorist whispers.

"I'm gonna get yoooooooooooou . . . I'm gonna get you with my pretty little kniiiiiiiiiiiife."

As he whispers I hear the blade scrape across the bathroom door.

SHHHUUUUUUUUKKKKKKK.

SHHHHUUUUUUUUUKKKKKKKK.

SHHHHHUUUUUUUUUUKKKKKKKKK.

SHHHHHHHHUUUUUUUUUKKKKKKKKKK.

"I'm gonna get yooooooooou with my pretttttty little kniiiiiiiiiiiife.

"Die, Die, Die, Die, Die, Die, Die, Die . . . Kill, Kill, Kill, Kill, Kill, Kill, Kill, Kill.

"Die, Die, Die, Die, Die, Die, Die, Die . . . Kill, Kill, Kill, Kill, Kill, Kill, Kill, Kill.

"Die, Die, Die, Die, Die, Die, Die, Die . . . Kill, Kill, Kill, Kill, Kill, Kill, Kill, Kill."

Heavy whispering. Breathing. Demonic whispers.

"Aaaaarrrraaaabeeeeeellllllaaaaaaa, I'm gonna get yooooooooou."

I stand on the toilet and pray for it to stop. I close my eyes and clasp my hands and I pray for it to stop and I shake. I shake and tremble and pray. I pray like I pray in my closet when I don't want to be in the house with Bill. I pray and beg and beg and beg. Please God, take me away. Please God, take me away. Please God, take me away.

I open my eyes and it is quiet. It is silent. There is no knife scraping.

I listen. I strain my ears and listen. Listen. Harder. And harder. And harder.

Nothing. There is no sound except for the rapid beats of my heart. The loud, rapid pounding in my chest and the ringing in my ears. The ringing in my ears and the loud pounding and the quick, shallow, begging breath. The desperation.

I think he's gone, but if I open the door he'll be there, I know it. I can't hear him, though.

I stand far from the door and drop to my hands and knees as quietly as I can.

I bring my face to the ground and I look. I search under the crack for any sign of his terror.

He is gone.

I hear the TV turn on.

I'm alone. He's done. He's done and he's going to leave me alone. He's going to leave me alone. He's going to leave me alone. I'm alone.

For now.

He'll be back. I know he'll be back. I breathe in less terror. Less horror. Less fear. But I know it's not over. He hasn't hurt me enough, so I know it's not over. I'm still scared because I know he will hurt me. It's not over.

Not yet.

And I'm stuck in this room. I look at the walls and the towels and the tub and the floor and feel Rage on top of terror. RAGE on top of TERROR.

I'm stuck in this tiny bathroom and it's sunny out and I want to go outside and jump on the trampoline.

RAGE.

I think about his whispers. His wanting to slice me up. Chasing me around the house with that slow, stalking stomp that Jason from Friday the 13th does. That's why he does it. He knows how much those movies scare me. He knows how scared I am of Jason. He knows how to scare me. He's a Terrorist.

As I sit on the toilet I look down at my thighs and think how disgusting they are. I should take the butcher knife from him and slice them all up and then he wouldn't have to hurt me.

I sit on the toilet and hear the TV and think about jumping on the trampoline. I think about being chased. RAGE and TERROR.

It's quiet except for the TV. He's down there and he's watching TV and he is waiting for me. Maybe I should try to escape. If I could get outside then he wouldn't chase me with the knife. He might punch me or something, but he wouldn't chase me with the knife. I don't think.

I sit in quiet and think of how scared I am. Scared. Scared. Scared.

I sit in quiet and think of how mad I am. Mad. Mad. Mad. I hate him. I really, really, really hate him. I'm all alone and I hate him. But at least he's not at the door.

SMASH!

"AAAAAAAAAAAHHHHHHHH!"

I jump in horror and scream bloody murder at the top of my lungs. My body shoots off of the toilet. My mind follows it. My heart stops. It stops. It stops. I can't breathe. I start to get dizzy and shake. I shake. I shake with fear and scream and I feel like I feel right before Bill hits me. I feel panic and fear and shake and shake and want to hide. I want to hide. I want to hide. I have to hide.

I look at the window and there he is. He's right up against the window with the knife. He's staring at me with his creepy I'm-going-to-kill-you look. He has the knife. The huge butcher knife that I use to chop up the salads. The huge butcher knife that he's going to gut me with. He's going to hold me down and kill me. He's going to take the knife and stab me in the chest and kill me.

Stabbing is the worst way to die. I don't want to die by a stabbing knife. I've seen it in the movies and it is the scariest way I can think of to die.

I breathe in short and quick. Suck in panic for breath.

Someone help me! I need help! Please someone stop this! My thoughts beg. Plead.

I'm going to die. I'm going to die. He's going to kill me. I want to hide. I want to hide. I want to die and then this won't happen anymore. It will be over, over, over, over, over.

He stares at me. He just stares with that look like he can't wait to kill me. He loves it. He feeds off of my fear. He's a psycho who only feels good when he tortures me. The more scared I am, the happier and more psycho his eyes look. He looks at me like murderers look at the women they are about to kill on the movies and TV.

Like the ones who like to strangle women. And as the women look scared and beg for their lives as they're being strangled, the murderers start to smile those evil smiles. That is Dave. He is the psycho strangler. I am the woman he will strangle.

So I wait.

I wait for him to strangle me. And then it will be over.

THIRTEEN YEARS OLD

I smell puke. I smell puke. I neeeeeeed water. I need water now. I can't move. Where am I? Shit, where am I?

I don't know where I am. I smell puke and there's a blanket over my face and my head is pounding. Throbbing. Throb. Throb. Throb. I need water. I can barely breathe because all I can smell is puke. The sour, nasty stench of puke. Fuck, it stinks.

I raise my hand to my face to rub my eye and I feel crustiness all over my cheek. I bring my other hand up to feel the other side and there is crust on it too. I am covered in crust. Fucking crust. Dried fucking something is crusted on my face.

I hear voices from below but I can't move to get up and get water. I need water. I need water. I need water. But I'm afraid to get up. I'm afraid to get up and find out where I am. Where the fuck am I? I need to know. I want to know. I don't want to know. I don't want to remember.

I'm afraid that the people who own the voices will tell me what I did last night. I wish I was dead. I wish I was fucking dead. I can't face them. I don't know who *them* are, but I can't do it. My fucking head throbs, I smell puke, and I am a fucking loser. I can't hear from someone else what I did. I can't take it one more time.

I'm staying under the blanket. I can't get up and find out what happened. I'm so thirsty though. I need to get up and get water and Advil. Or weed. Something to make this constant throbbing stop. Throbbing and thirst. Every throb sucks out another drop of fluid from my veins. Need Water. I need fucking water now.

I roll over onto my side but I stay under the covers. My ribs hurt. As I roll, my ribs feel like they're being crushed. Someone has crushed my ribs. My ribs are gone. Someone broke them. Something happened. Oh God; what the fuck happened last night?

I need to fucking puke. God, I feel so sick. I want to die. I want to fucking die.

I have to open my eyes. OPEN YOUR FUCKING EYES, ARABELLA!!!

Just do it. Open your eyes. Open them. Open them. OPEN THEM NOW!

I can't open them because then I'll see where I am and what has happened.

FLASH!

I am outside of Ramie's sister's house. There is hard, crusty snow on the ground. I see my stepsister walking up the road and I yell hi to her. As I yell, I topple over the fence that I am leaning on. I fall and everyone laughs. I fall and everyone laughs at me. Because I'm a loser.

Everyone laughs because I'm a fucking loser. I am a fucking drunk loser. I'm a fucking loser and I want to die. Everyone knows what a loser

I am. They all know and I still can't stop. I can't stop. I'm a loser and I can't stop . . .

I have to open my eyes. I have to do it. Just do it. I make myself. Through the throbbing and the pounding and the withering and the aching, I force myself to open them.

I open them and I stay under the covers. It's light enough for me to see myself.

I look down. There's dried crusty orange and yellow puke on my shirt and on my pants. The backs of my hands are covered in puke.

I reach up to feel my hair. There are moist chunks sticking in it. Fresh, squishy, rank-smelling chunks in my hair.

I want to die. I want to fucking die. I want to fucking die. I am such a loser. A fucking loser that no one likes. They all hate me because I do this. FUCKING HATE ME!

I am *not* like my friends. I drink and don't stop. I can't stop. I need it. I think about it all the time. But I hate myself every time I do it. Like right now.

I fucking hate myself. I'm a loser who can't hold her liquor like her friends.

I drink and drug and do the most of whatever I can and I don't want to stop. I can't stop. I need it. I need it and I hate it. I hate it and I hate myself. I hate myself. But I need it.

FLASH!

Sean and Tyson are standing in the kitchen with me. I have a bottle of Jim Beam. I'm pouring mugfuls for them.

I'm so attracted to them. Both of them. I want both of them, but especially Sean. I've had a crush on him since I met him. He's Autumn's boyfriend, so he's off-limits. He's the perfect man. He's the perfect man and if he was my boyfriend I would finally be happy . . .

FLASH!

"I can out-drink you both."

"Yeah right, Arabella. We have five years and about fifty pounds each on you."

"I bet you I can drink three full mugs of Jim Beam straight."

"Good luck. I don't think I can drink two mugs."

"Me either, Sean. Go ahead and try it, Arabella, but I really doubt you can do it."

"Oh, I can do it. I can drink the two of you under the table." . . .

Oh God. I stood in the kitchen and drank the mugs of Jim Beam. I did it to try to impress Sean and Tyson. I did it because I wanted to be around them. I wanted them to notice me. I just wanted them to notice me. I want to be noticed. I need to be noticed. I have to . . . be . . . noticed.

I have to be noticed by Sean. He's so hot and I want him to want me. Even though I can't go out with him. Even though he's Autumn's boyfriend. Even though he's too old for me, I want him to notice me. I want his attention. He's so cute and I just want him to notice me.

I lay and think. I lay and think about Sean. I think about Sean and I endure the throbs and the stench and the warmth between my legs. Why is it warm between my legs?

Oh fuck. I fucking pissed myself again. I fucking pissed myself. I can't get up. I can't get out of here. I have to get out of here. I am so disgusting. I'm a fucking loser who pukes and pisses and sleeps in her fucking bodily fluids. I'm fucking disgusting.

I throb and berate and condemn. I condemn myself. I berate myself. I'm everything despicable in the world. I am disgusting. No one fucking likes me.

Everyone knows what a loser I am and I need to die. I have to die. I might as well die because no one likes me. I hate myself. HATE. HATE. HATE. HATE.

I condemn because I am nothing. I berate because I am nothing. I am despicable and I deserve nothing. I deserve all of this shit that I want to die over. I deserve nothing good because I *am* nothing. Nothing.

No thing.

TWENTY-TWO YEARS OLD

I look over at Kallie and she looks back at me.

"You ready?"

She gives me a knowing smile and says she's as ready as she'll ever be.

We both look down at the glass table. My glass table. My marble dining room table with glass on top of it. It is our Mecca.

Nothing else really exists. Just me, her, and the table. Me, her, and the table. Me and her. The table. The table. Table. Table. Table.

Neither of us have done this before. I'm nervous and I tell her. She tells me she's nervous too.

We banter to stall. Nervous banter. Uneasy chitchat. The kind you do when there's an uncomfortable moment and you're doing everything you can to make it more comfortable. But the chitchat just makes it more uncomfortable. That's what we do. Try too hard to make an uncomfortable moment comfortable and end up making it more uncomfortable.

I don't know what we're uncomfortable about. We've been friends for a while. We're comfortable with each other. We live together. We know each other. We like each other. And we're friends.

It'll be fine. It's going to be fine. It'll be fun. Really fun.

As we both stare at the table, I ask if she's ready.

She says, "Let's do it."

So we do.

We do it at the same time.

And the moment is exactly like we heard it would be.

The feeling as the straw goes into the nostril.

The stinging as it shoots in through the nostril and to the back of the throat.

The stinging. The fucking stinging. STINGING!

The slow numbing feeling in the back of the throat.

And the drip. The first slow drip.

Drip.

Chemicals.

Drip. Drip.

Ajax.

Then quicker.

Drip, drip, drip, drip, drip of the chemicals and Ajax into the throat.

The moment is exactly like we heard it would be, except for one small detail.

The gagging.

Kallie looks at me with a contorted face and says, "Oh God; I'm gonna puke."

She runs into the bathroom and I hear the toilet seat smash against the tank. And then retching.

She's retching.

"AAAAAGGGGGGHHHHHHH!"

I hear gagging and retching and contracting. I hear the heaves and the Ahhhhhggggggghhhhhhhggggggggggghhhhhhhh! I hear her chewed-up lunch hitting the water in small, spaced-out splashes. SPLASHES.

I run into the bathroom to hold back her hair. I stand behind and over her and pull her hair out of the way.

SPLASH!

"Oh my God, Bella!"

SPLASH!

"The fucking taste!"

SPLASH!

"I can't fucking stand the taste!"

SPLASH!

"I'm . . . gonna . . . be throwing . . . up . . . all night!"

SPLASH!

"My fucking throat!"

SPLASH!

"WHY DID WE DO THIS? FUUUUCK!"

As I stand above her and hold her hair and smell the stench of the splash, I feel the contractions start. My muscles start to flex and I start to taste the chemicals in my throat.

In small drips. I taste a mix of Ajax and aspirin. Chemicals. Fucking chemicals. All I can taste is chemicals.

And now it's my turn. I can't help it. All of her heaving and retching and splashing of lunch in the water and my abs start to contract more. I start to gag.

"Kallie!"

GAG!

"I have to puke!"

GAG!

"I'm gonna fucking puke!"

GAG!

She tells me she can't move; she's not done.

"Fuck!"

GAG!

"Oh my God!"

GAG!

"I'm gonna fucking puke!"

I run into the kitchen and just as I reach the sink I vomit. All over. My lunch and aspirin and Ajax and no SPLASH.

I stand and contract and puke and feel my nose getting numb. The back of my throat getting numb. Dripping numbing puking.

"AAhhggggggggggghhhhhhhhggggggggggaaaaahhhhhggggggg! Fuck, Kallie! This is fucking gross!"

I stare at the sink. And feel the contractions subside.

I turn on the faucet to rinse the chunks of aspirin and Ajax and lunch down the drain. I'm done. It's gone. Out of my system. I can't feel the back of my throat and the insides of my nostrils are clear and open and numb.

As it starts to hit me and the taste is disappearing, I hear Kallie retch again.

SPLASH!

This time it's more severe, more painful sounding, and more repulsive. More contagious. And again I start.

Heaving. Retching. Barfing. Vomiting. Contracting. Chunks. Liquid. Liquid. Liquid. Ajax. Aspirin. Chemicals. Chemicals. Fucking Chemicals. Fucking Crank.

I hear Kallie yell, "You have to stop . . ."

RETCH

". . . fucking . . ."

GAG

". . . puking . . ."

RETCH

". . . Bella."

GAG

". . . I can . . ."

RETCH

". . . hear it . . ."

". . . and you're . . ."

RETCH . . . RETCH . . . RETCH

". . . making me . . ."

". . . puke more . . ."

As I stand over the sink and continue retching, I hear it hit her again. She contracts. SPLASHES. Smaller now. There isn't much left. Just liquid. Only liquid and Ajax and aspirin and nasty, foamy spit. The foamy spit that is only produced by retching of this kind. By chemicals. Chemical retching and chemical contracting.

This goes on for what seems like hours. She's in the bathroom and I'm in the kitchen. Hearing the other retch and gagging in response. Retching because of the retching in the next room. Chemicals and liquid and retching and gagging and retching and gagging.

After a few moments there is silence. There is silence except for sniffling and deep breaths. Deep breaths of relief. Silence. The kind of silence that occurs in suspense.

Silence.

Breaths.

Silence.

Breaths.

Relief.

And it's over.

"Are you okay, Bella?"

"Yeah, are you?"

"Yeah. Fuck. Wasn't expecting that, huh?"

"Fuck no. That fucking sucked. But I'm starting to feel it, how 'bout you?"

"Oh yeah."

I walk into the bathroom and we see each other and laugh. We laugh and we laugh and we laugh and we laugh and we laugh.

We laugh so hard that tears stream down our faces. We laugh so hard that we fold over and grab our knees. We laugh so hard that we brace ourselves on the countertop. We laugh so hard that we can't breathe.

And we finish getting ready for another night out on the town. And we laugh some more the whole time we do. Because we're friends and because our puke contest was really fucking funny.

TWENTY-SEVEN YEARS OLD

As I pull my truck up to the mailboxes, I grab the keys out of the console.

I put the gold one into the keyhole and grab the stack of papers.

I sift through them as I always do when I pick up the mail.

Junk.

Weekly Press.

Grocery coupons.

Gas bill.

Electric bill.

Insurance bill.

And a white envelope. A small white envelope that's handwritten and addressed to Arabella Winters. The handwriting is just like mine.

The return address is none other than Rachel Rowers. My mother. My mother. My mother.

I haven't heard from her since she hung the phone up on me a couple years ago.

FLASH!

My brother has just gotten out of jail and my grandmother has driven from Kansas to welcome him home. I think that I should call and say hello to him, so I do . . . .

I look at the envelope with a surge of longing and excitement. Maybe this is it. Maybe she's finally going to be here for me. Maybe she's writing to tell me that she loves me and wants to be here for me. Maybe she's writing because she wants to tell me how sorry she is for everything that she's done. Maybe she's really sorry. Maybe she's sorry and she finally wants to be here for me. Maybe I'm finally going to have a mother.

I drive into the driveway and park. I grab the stack of mail and walk inside. I sit at my marble dining room table and start to open the mail. Not hers, though.

I save hers for last. I save hers for last because I like to save the best for last. This is what I do with my mail and this is what I do with my food. I open—and eat—the stuff that isn't the best first. And I think about the best that I'm saving the whole time that I eat and open the worst. Then I have something to look forward to.

I stare at the little white envelope. I can see a small piece of yellow paper inside. A little yellow paper inside. I anticipate. Contemplate. Speculate. Hope. Imagine. Dream. Long. Crave. Need.

This is what I do anytime I think of my mother. It's nothing new.

FLASH!

I call and my brother answers. I haven't spoken to him in about a year or so. And the conversation is exactly like it is every time we speak. I ask questions and he answers with the most complete answers he thinks I deserve.

I ask how he is.

"Fine."

I ask if it is nice to be home.

"Yeah."

I ask what his plans are.

"I don't know."

UNCOMFORTABLE SILENCE. As usual. I've always tried to be close with him. But he has always hated me and treated me like I was a loser. Less than him. Stupid. Annoying. Stupid. Stupid. Stupid.

I start to tell him about school. About me being in college. Proud of myself. Trying to connect with him. Get him to see me. Get him to be proud of me. Get him to like me. Get him to love me. Get him to say something nice to me. Get him to say something.

He says that he heard I had straight As. Then he says, "Who would've thought that you could do that? Who'd a thought that you could get good grades?"

STUPID!

Then he says that he heard that I got a new truck. And he follows that by saying that I am a yuppie brat. I live on the water and go to college and have an SUV.

STUPID! LESS THAN HIM! LOSER!

I feel like he just punched me in the stomach. I try to connect with him and tell him how I'm doing and he always puts me down. He always hurts me. He knocks the wind out of me with his pounding, harsh words.

It's always the same. I'm stupid and a loser and annoying and not as good as him. It's always the same. I end up feeling like the beat-up little girl he used to torture with his fists and knives and words.

I ask him if I can speak to Mom and instead my grandmother gets on the phone. She has no interest in me. She just tells me how excited she is that the man who walks on water is out of jail. How she drove all the way to Montana to see him. How he this and how he that. No questions about me.

The Rage starts to well up inside of me. The RAGE that I feel every time I hear the word "grandma" or "grandmother." RAGE. RAGE. RAGE. I want to smack her in the face. I want to kick my brother in his kneecaps.

I want to scream at them, I'M RIGHT HERE! SEE ME?!?!? I'M RIGHT FUCKING HERE! LOOK WHAT'S GOING ON WITH ME!!!

But I don't. I sink into that feeling of worthlessness and pain and RAGE and invisible. I am invisible. I am stupid and worthless and invisible and fucking pissed.

I ask to speak to my mom. She's the only one who I think I may have a chance with. I hold out hope that she'll save me.

She gets on the phone and I ask her if she could talk to me for a minute. I tell her I'm upset and I really need to talk.

She says she has company.

I ask her if she would take the phone and go outside or upstairs and talk to me. I really need to talk to her.

She says, "No, I have company."

I say, "You can't take a minute to talk to me? What about your promise to be here for me? When you came out here for therapy?!?!? Less than a month ago?!?!?!"

She says, "You're acting like a baby," and hangs up.

She hangs up and that's the last time I speak to her for a long time . . .

I stare at the envelope. I stare at the little envelope with an older version of my handwriting on it. I stare at the spelling and the address and the curves of her W and her A. I stare at them and feel RAGE. Pain. Alone. Long. Crave. Need. Pain. Hurt. Longing. Longing. Need. Hope. Hope. Hope. HOPE. HOPE. HOPE. HOPE. HOPE. HOPE. HOPE. HOPE. HOPE.

I start to tear the back envelope flap open, slowly and methodically. I'm waiting for the news. The news that she's ready to be my mom. The news that she's ready to love me. The news that she's ready to see me. The news that she's going to love me like she loves my brother. The news that I'm visible. She's going to see me and love me.

I open it and pull out the small yellow piece of paper. One piece of paper. One. One. One. The size of a large Post-it Note. One piece of paper the size of a large Post-it Note.

The disappointment rolls over me. It rolls over me like a cement truck. It rolls over me like I'm an ant and I am nothing. I am nothing. I am nothing. I am nothing.

I'm hit like I am every time I have encounters with my mother. I hope and long and pray and need and crave and cry and pray and hope and long and need. And every time it's the same. Every time I still hope. The hope is always there. It never leaves. It's all that I have. Hope.

I read the words and everything around me starts to disappear. Sounds are gone. Smell is gone. My animals are gone. The house is gone. The sun is gone. Everything else is gone.

Everything disappears. Everything disappears and I'm thrust into a tiny, dismal gap where nothing else exists but the letter and me. And I read the words. I read them again. And again and again:

Arabella,

Bill Rowers had a heart attack and died about a month ago. He was fifty-four. I thought that I should be the one to tell you. I miss you . . .

I read it again and again and again and again and again.

I'm in the tiny, little, dismal, suffocating gap where nothing else exists. I don't feel and I don't know any words except: What? "What" with a question mark. Nothing makes sense. I am in a tiny, dismal, suffocating, hopeless gap where nothing makes sense.

It's just me and the letter and the dejection of the gap.

NINE TO THIRTEEN YEARS OLD

House on Bear Street

"YOU FUCKING IDIOT! WHAT IS WRONG WITH YOU!?!?! HUH!?!?!"

SMACK!

"NOTHING. NO! NO! NOTHING, BILL! NOTHING!"

I'm upstairs and I hear screaming and shoving and pounding and the sound of a body being thrown against a wall. I hear Bill screaming. I hear my brother wailing. Crying. Begging. Pleading. Wailing. Being hit. Being Smacked. Pounded. Thrown. Hurt.

I start to cry. I start to bawl. I must save my brother. I must do something to save my brother. I have to save him. He's crying and being hit and he didn't do anything. I have to save him. He's my big brother and I love him and I want to save him.

"YOU FUCKING IDIOT! I'M GONNA TEACH YOU A FUCKING LESSON!"

Crying and pleading and begging and smacking and throwing and pleading.

I run downstairs. I can't see through my tears and I slip on the stairs on the way down. I slip because I want to save him. I slip because I feel his pain. I slip because I want to be the one being hit instead of him. I slip because I have seen the terror on his face. The desperate look of being betrayed. The look of agony. The look of grief and the look of anguish. I slip because I love him and he is my big brother. I slip because he doesn't deserve what he is getting.

I walk through the living room and I'm shaking. I am shaking and scared and I need to save him. I am sick. My stomach is flipping. FLIPPING. SWIRLING. TURNING. TWISTING.

I need to save him. I hear him cry out in pain as a blow hits his body. I hear the sound of Bill's fist hit his body as I reach the bedroom door.

Crying. Begging. Pleading. Pain. Anguish. Betrayal. Confusion. Grief and Terror. Terror. His cries are loaded with terror. And confusion.

And the threats and taunts are filled with RAGE and FURY and CONDEMNATION.

"YOU FUCKING IDIOT!"

SMACK!

"YOU FUCKING IDIOT!"

WHACK!

"YOU FUCKING IDIOT!"

POUND!

"YOU FUCKING LITTLE SHIT!"

SMACK! SMACK!

As I turn the corner I see Bill pounding on Dave. Bill is in the doorway and he's as tall as the door. He is as tall as the door and my brother is as small as a GI Joe. He is tiny and curled and huddled and his hands are above his head. And Bill is pounding him. Pounding him hard. There are tears and cries and RAGE and POUNDING and THUMPING.

All over his little GI Joe head. He is being beaten on his head and his face and his arms and his neck and his stomach and he is a helpless GI Joe and Bill is a building. He is smashing him.

I stand and cry. I stand frozen and cry silent tears. I cry and look and I am lost. I don't know what to do. I don't know what to do and I have to save him. I have to save him because I love him and he's my brother and I have to save him.

I'm frozen. I am frozen watching my big brother shrink from the blows.

"YOU FUCKING IDIOT!"

WHACK!

Crying. Shrinking. Aching. Bewilderment. Fear. Terror. Betrayal. Betrayal. Betrayal.

I watch, frozen, as Bill backs him into the corner and beats on him and shoves him and throws him against the wall. Dave hits the wall and Bill starts to smack him and punch him and scream at him and berate him and hurt him and RAGE and pain and terror and betrayal.

I stand frozen and cry. I cry. I can't move. I am stuck standing in the hall and I wail. I watch my big brother shrink into Bill's RAGE. Begging and pleading and aching. And needing to be rescued.

He looks up and sees me. He yells for me to GO AWAY!

He doesn't yell because he wants me to escape a beating. He yells because he is ashamed. He is embarrassed. He wants to hide and he wants to disappear. He doesn't want me to see his helplessness. He doesn't want me to see him being humiliated and berated and condemned and smacked and punched and kicked and hurt and the object of the RAGE.

I stand frozen and cry. I see his arms above him. He's crying in desperation. Begging. Pleading. Curled into a corner. Arms overhead. Desperately trying to block the blows. Frantically trying to shrink into the cracks of the wall behind him. Tears. No. Not tears. A howling river pounding his cheeks. His shirt. His pants. His soul. Pounding him. Beating him. Betraying him.

I stand frozen and cry. All I see is his face. That look. That look. That look that will never be erased from my mind.

The look of desperate anguish. The look of shame. SHAME. SHAME. SHAME. The look of being betrayed. The look of being wrongly persecuted. The look of complete and utter disbelief and betrayal. The look of being alone. The look of being alone. The look that he cannot be saved. The look that longs for saving.

The look that I will see on his face again.

SEVENTEEN YEARS OLD

"THE COPS ARE HERE! THE COPS ARE FUCKING HERE!"

Oh shit! The fucking cops! Panic. Panic. Panic. Fuck. Fuck. Fuck.

"WHAT THE FUCK ARE WE GOING TO DO?"

I look to my brother for an answer. Search his eyes.

There are kids scattering everywhere. Kids running up the stairs. Kids bolting out the door. Kids grabbing their beer out of the fridge and kids grabbing their bottles off of the counter and running outside. Taking off to hide from the cops.

Life will be over if we're caught with booze. We have to do something but the cops have blocked all of the cars in. The fucking cop cars are blocking all of the cars in the driveway.

"What are we going to do, Dave?"

Fuck. Fuck. Fuck. We have to run. We have to take off out into the woods and run.

"Grab the beer and let's go, Arabella."

POUND. POUND. POUND.

The cops are at the door.

There's panic and chaos and running and freaking out. Everywhere I look there are kids fleeing and panicking and freaking out.

"LET'S GET THE FUCK OUT OF HERE, ARABELLA!"

I look over at my brother and his eyes are urgent. They are urgent and demanding and ready to run. He wants to run. He wants to run out the door into the snow. The feet of snow. I have moccasins on and I can't go running in the snow. I don't have any beer. The cops are already inside and he wants me to run in the fucking snow.

"I'm staying here, Dave."

"NO! YOU HAVE TO COME WITH ME, ARABELLA!"

"No, I'm staying. The cops are already here. I have moccasins on and I'm not running in feet of snow."

His best friend looks at me and looks at him and says, "She's right, dude. We should just stay here."

Dave looks at me with RAGE. He looks like he wants to blow. His face starts to contort into the evil FUCK-YOU look that he gets when he wants to hurt me. He's gonna snap. I see the desperate look that he gets when he's going snap. The same look Bill gets. He needs to hit me. He needs to hurt me. He has to hit me. He has to hurt. Me. Nothing exists for him but hurting me. I am what he needs to hit and hurt and humiliate and RAGE on.

Thank God there are people around. Thank God. He can't hurt me with all of these people arou—

THUD! THUD! THUD!

My jaw slams shut and my teeth collide in my mouth. The top of my head suddenly swells in agony. Pain. I'm dizzy. Vibrate. My teeth vibrate. I can't stand. I need to sit. I see stars. My jaw. My fucking jaw. I think my teeth are all broken.

My teeth and my jaw and my head. Throb. Pound. Ache. Vibrate pain ache pound thud. I can't stand. I need to sit. I need to sit. I can't stand. I'm dizzy. I'm fucking dizzy.

Stars. Stars. Little white spots flying all around me. Flying white spots. Green spots. Spots floating in front of my eyes. I need to sit. I can't see. Fucking stars and haze and spots and I need to sit.

I'm going to fucking pass out. My teeth. My fucking teeth. My fucking head. The top of my head feels as if a sledgehammer has cracked it open. My fucking head is split open. My fucking head is broken. My skull is cracked. Cracked fucking open. Pain. Pain. Pain. I wait for blood to drip down. I feel my head splitting and wait for the blood to drip down.

"WHAT THE FUCK, DAVE? WHAT THE FUCK DID YOU JUST HIT YOUR SISTER FOR?"

I feel someone grab my arm and ask if I'm okay.

"Are you okay, Arabella?"

I can't see. I can't fucking see anything except for stars.

The person holding my arm sits me in a chair. I'm in a chair and I see stars. In front of me I see his figure. My savior. Through the stars I see him. I hear him ask me if I'm okay. I see the boy that I have loved since I was in the fourth grade. Through the pain and the stars and the throbbing in my mouth, and the cracking of my skull, and the swelling of my brain, and the overwhelming dizziness, and the tears that stream as a bodily reaction to being pounded and not from pain, I see him. My savior. I see him. Jake. And he Sees me.

He sees my shame. He sees my pain. He sees my humiliation. He Sees me. HE SEES ME. That is why I love him and have loved him since I met him when I was nine years old.

As I come into focus and realize that Dave beat the top of my head like he was playing that game at the carnival—the one where you're given a mallet and you have to beat the heads of gophers as they pop out of their holes—I hear voices everywhere. There are cops all around.

I hear the cops give Dave a ticket. I hear them give him a ticket for having beer. An MIP. A Minor in Possession. He gets a ticket and I get pounded in the head like a gopher. He pounds me in the head like a gopher because he knows that he will get a ticket.

I deserve to be pounded in the head because he got a ticket. I'm a fucking shit for not going with him. It's my fucking fault.

But I still hate him. I feel sorry for him and I hate him. I hate him for hitting me and humiliating me and pounding my head. I feel sorry for him for getting a ticket.

I'll fix it, though.

I sneak outside. Somehow I sneak past the cops and go outside. I have to do something. I don't know what, but I have to do something to fix this. To show those stupid fucking pigs. Those fucking pigs. If it weren't for those stupid fucking pigs, Dave wouldn't have gotten a ticket.

I walk down the cold driveway. The snowy driveway. I'm furious. The top of my head is throbbing and my teeth feel broken and my jaw feels cracked and I am waiting for the blood to start dripping down my face. I walk in the cold in my RAGE and pain. Excruciating pain and RAGE. RAGE. PAIN. RAGE. PAIN. RAGE. RAGE. PAINFUL, FUCKING RAGE!

I walk in the snow and I'm looking for their stupid fucking cop cars. I look for their stupid, fucking, white cop cars. I'll do something. I have to do something. I have to get rid of this RAGE. The fucking RAGE that the fucking pigs make me feel. I must fuck them up. I'm going to fuck them up.

I'll show them. I'll teach them who they can give an MIP to. Fucking pigs! I'll fucking show them!

I walk down the driveway and see the cars. Their fucking white pig cars. I want to smash all of the lights in. I want to bust the windows open. I want to release all of the RAGE that is making my heart pound and my head throb and my teeth ache. I want to smash the humiliation away. I want to break it open and do it for my brother. I want to kick through the metal for his MIP. I want to bust and break and freak out. I need to freak out. I have to freak out. I have to get revenge. I have to do something to them for giving him a fucking ticket.

As I walk around the cars and wait for the RAGE to guide me, I hear whispers in the trees and whispers down the drive and whispers up the drive.

Whispers asking me if the cops are gone.

"NO! THEY'RE STILL HERE AND THEY GAVE MY BROTHER A FUCKING TICKET AND I'M GOING TO FUCK THEIR CARS UP!!"

Now I have an audience. I have an audience to egg me on. I have a witness. I have a witness to my RAGE and my pain and my vengeance and my throbbing and aching and pain. I have a witness to see the blood when it starts to drip down my face. I have a witness for me to break and shatter and bust and smash and pound.

I look into one of the cars and see a huge rifle hanging on the gate that separates the front from the back seat. I want the fucking rifle. I have to get the rifle so that I can blow the fucking lights off of the top of the car. The fucking red and white and blue lights. Blow them to smithereens.

Blow the fucking tires off. Blow the fucking windows out. I have to get the rifle and blow up the car because they gave Dave the MIP. And I'm going to show them who they can fuck with. FUCK THEM! FUCK THE FUCKING PIGS!

As I look into the window, I decide I'll try to open the door.

HOLY FUCK!

It opens.

Those fucking idiots didn't even lock the fucking doors. Fucking morons. What fucking idiots. Now they're fucked.

I reach in and realize that I can't get to the gun. The front doors are locked. Only the back ones are open.

FUCK! FUCK! FUCK!

Now I can't get the fucking rifle and blow the hell out of their cars.

Think. Think, Arabella. What can I do? What can I do? What can I do to fuck them up like they fucked up my brother?

That's when I see them. Three of them. One in each car. Three of them. Fucking three of them! Perfect.

Pigs are so fucking stupid. Fucking idiots. And I'll show them.

I scream up the driveway.

"FUCK YOU, PIGS!!"

I hear whispered giggles in the trees and up the driveway and down the driveway. I laugh.

Fuck yeah. My blood is pumping. My heart is racing. I'm ready to do some damage. I feel fucking high and higher. I feel fucking good. I feel ready and high and I'm going to do some damage to their pretty little egos.

The pain in my head and my teeth and my jaw and my pride is fading into the background. Smothered by adrenaline. Smothered by vengeance. Smothered by the giggles egging me on in the trees.

So I do it.

I walk up to each car and open the door and take out a flight jacket from each one. I take a fuzzy, fucking, pig skin from each car.

I take their pride. And I leave them with humiliation and questions.

I leave with my vengeance and my pride.

I leave behind my humiliation and RAGE.

NINE YEARS OLD

I pull on the slats of the doors and shut both of them. It is darker in here than it is out in my bedroom. It's darker, but safer.

I sit and stare at the shelves. I stare at my sweaters on the shelves. I stare at my clothes hanging above my head. I stare at my shoes that I moved to the end so that I could lay out my Holly Hobby blanket.

I like it in here. It's safe. This is the only safe place. I have my teddy bears and my Cabbage Patch dolls and my Holly Hobby blanket and my pillow and it's safe. Safer than out there.

For now it is safe. There is no blood and no punches. No bruises and no screaming. No butcher knives and no fists. No kicks and no mean words. For now it is safe. Because I am alone.

It's safe in here until I hear Bill's loud truck. Then he's home and I don't know what will happen next. I don't know what will happen cuz he's really mean. He's mean and I don't ever know what he will do to me. I sit in here cuz this is where the angels are. This is where my dolls are and this is where I feel safest.

I know in here no one can get me. It will be harder for them to get me. They will have to look for me in here. And then maybe while they look, they will give up. They will give up and forget about me. And I can stay in here with my dolls and my angels. My dolls and my angels. And God too. Mom said God is everywhere so God is in here too. Maybe he'll have an easier time finding me in here.

I hate it here. I hate living in this house. I hate it. I hate Bill and he's mean. He's mean and my brother's mean. My mom is only nice when she has her pink cup in the garage. She only has time for me when I go to the garage and watch her drink and tell her everything is going to be okay. I tell her everything will be good.

I clasp my hands like we do in church and I ask God to please take me away.

God, please make it better.

God, please take it away.

God, please make it stop.

I'll be good.

I promise if you take it away I will be good.

God, please make someone come and take it away.

God, pleeeeease make it better. Make it all better and I swear I will be good.

God, please make Dave stop scaring me and hitting me.

God, please make Bill stop scaring us and hitting us.

God, please make my mom leave him.

God, please take it all away and come get me.

God, please. If you come get me I promise I will never ever be bad.

I cross my heart and hope to die. And then I'll stick a needle in my eye.

FIFTEEN YEARS OLD

I stand in front of my mirror. The mirror in my bedroom. My full-length mirror that I leaned up against the wall. I look into the mirror and I stare at all of the disgusting fat that's taken over my body.

I am fucking disgusting. Fucking sickening. Fucking fat and gross and I want to cut all of the fat off of my body.

I can't eat. I can't eat because I am gross and fat and none of my friends look like me. I am disgusting. I just want to look like a model. I want to be skinny like the models in my mom's magazines. I want to be skinny like the women on TV.

I want to be skinny and small like my mom.

As I stare at the fat the RAGE starts to take over.

FLASH!

I'm in the kitchen making dinner.

I take a tortilla and start to put peanut butter on it. I get the jelly out and get ready to put some of that on the tortilla too.

My mom walks up behind me.

"You know, Arabella, there are a lot of calories in that peanut butter. It would be better if you put mushrooms on that. Then you wouldn't gain weight."

"Thanks, Mom" . . .

I look in the mirror and feel the RAGE take over. I want to freak out. I want to scream. I want to rip my skin off. I want to cut the skin off so that I don't have to look at how fucking disgusting I am. I am a fat fucking pig.

I feel disgusting and fat and huge and wrong and I wish I could cut the fat off of my huge thighs and then I'd be happy. I'd be happy if I could take the disgusting fat of my huge ass and my huge thighs and cut it off.

Then I'd be happy. If I were skinny then I'd be happy. I wouldn't have to worry about anything. I could be like Ramie and eat anything and not gain weight and be happy and guys would like me and I wouldn't hate myself.

I could focus on other stuff. Ramie never worries about her weight. She never ever worries about it and she doesn't care because she's skinny. If I could just be skinny, then I wouldn't have anything to worry about. I'd be happy.

I fucking hate myself. And the RAGE wells up. It's swelling and with each swell my thighs expand and my ass expands and my stomach expands and I want to freak out and cut my skin off.

FLASH!

I'm on my mom's stationary bicycle. I have to workout so that I can become skinny and happy.

My brother drives up with his friends. He drives up and gets out and before I have a chance to leave the room they all come in. They sit on the couch and watch the TV that I have on while I workout.

As I get off the bike to go to my bedroom I hear Jerry say, "No wonder you're working out, look at your thighs" . . .

I stare in the mirror and condemn and berate and the rage surges through my body. I feel my heart running. Racing.

I turn to make sure that the bedroom door is locked. It is.

I stare at the mirror and grab my growing thighs. I grab them and twist them and I pinch the fat. I want to fucking rip it off of my body. I want to kill it. I want to fucking twist and pinch and slice and kill it. I want to tear it off so that it'll stop looking at me in the mirror. It'll stop telling me how fucking gross I am.

FLASH!

Me and my mom stand in front of the BIG mirror above our couch. We stand in front of the mirror and she starts the ceremonial comparisons.

She puts her arm around me and starts to laugh. Her annoying fucking laugh.

"Look how BIG you are compared to me! I'm so small compared to you! I look like a little midget compared to you! YOU ARE SO BIG, ARABELLA! AND I AM SO SMALL COMPARED TO YOU! LOOK! LOOK AT US!"

COMPARE! COMPARE! FUCKING COMPARE!

With each comparison my reflection gets BIGger and BIGGER and my spirit gets smaller and smaller. I am nothing . . .

I stare at the mirror with the fat in my hands and twist. I twist and cry. I don't cry from pain. I cry a raging cry. That I can't change the fat. That I'm not small. That I'm BIG and disgusting. That I don't have the courage to cut the fat from my thighs. That I am no one and nothing. That I'm not someone else. That I'm stuck in this disgusting body that no one wants. A cry that no matter how hard I twist I still have to look at the disgusting fat on my thighs in the morning.

FLASH!

I'm on the school bus. I'm sitting in the back seat and I'm eating a Nutty Bar ice cream cone.

Rick, the guy that all of the girls want because he's popular and cute, gets on and sits in front of me.

He looks at me eating my ice cream cone and says, "You don't need that" . . .

I'm fucking repulsive and everyone thinks so. Fucking sick and repulsive and fat and disgusting.

The only reason that guys sleep with me is because I will. I'm fat and gross and no guys ever like me for me. They just want to fuck me when they're drunk and forget about my fat in the morning.

I cry and cry and twist the fat. I know in the morning there'll be bruises there.

And I know that no matter how hard I twist, the fat will be there too.

TWENTY-SIX YEARS OLD

I cry and look down in shame. I cry and look down in shame as I talk to her.

I grab a box of Kleenex and finish telling her about one of those times.

I look at her and tell her I must have been around eleven or twelve, because my aunt and uncle were living in this one house where I remember being at that age.

I stare out the window and remember.

FLASH!

I wake up to a creak from the floor.

I rub my eyes and remember where I am.

I am lying in bed at my cousin's house. We're in Jessica's room and I'm sharing the bed with her. I think that maybe her hand hit me in her sleep.

I roll over and see that she's on the other side of the bed.

I go back to sleep thinking that it must've been a dream.

I wake up again and I feel something on my waist. I shoot straight up in the bed and I look around the dark room. Whatever was there is gone.

I wake up Jessica. I nudge her. I whisper that I just felt something touch me and she tells me it's nothing and to go back to sleep.

I lie back down and try to go back to sleep and I see a shadow at the end of the room. It's tall and I'm terrified. Fear. Panic. Terror. My heart starts to thump louder and louder and I'm afraid that the shadow will hear.

There's someone in the room and I'm terrified. I don't know what to do. I'm frozen. I'm frozen and all I feel is terror and panic and fear and panic and terror. Thump. Thump. Thump. Thumpthumpthumpthumpthumpthump. My heart threatens to burst through my chest.

There is a huge shadow at the end of the room at the end of the bed and I'm frozen. It starts to move. It starts to move closer. Closer to the end of the bed. It moves to Jessica's side.

I am terrified. I feel fear. I am frozen. I feel something on my waist.

I roll over towards Jessica. I nudge her.

She wakes up.

I whisper in her ear that there are people in the room. I tell her I just felt something touch me and I tell her that I saw a shadow walk into the room and come up next to her side of the bed.

She is scared. I am scared. We are scared. We lay frozen. Frozen, both of us. Frozen in our fear and to the bed. We are frozen to the bed. Frozen and we can't move.

Suddenly a hand reaches up and touches my butt. I suck in a fearful gasp. At the same time Jessica sucks in a gasp.

We hear a giggle.

We suck in and don't scream. We suck in and don't scream because we know who it is. We know that it's our brothers who want to touch us in the night . . .

I stare out the window and feel the shame override all other feelings. Shame and disgust and shame and humiliation. I want to disappear into the couch. I'm disgusting and repulsive.

I feel like she thinks that it wasn't really abuse. I don't even know if I believe it was. I can't even say the words "sexual abuse" when I refer to it. I call it "when he used to do stuff to me." I'm fucking disgusting. Fucking disgusting because I didn't scream or hit or fight him off.

I glance at her quickly to determine whether or not she thinks I'm a BIG, fucking cousin-fucker who liked it.

She just looks at me with love. I continue.

"I . . . I don't know what was wrong with me. I should've just gotten up and screamed 'Get the fuck out of the room!' I don't know why I didn't. Instead we just lay there frozen to the bed and rolled towards each other. We rolled towards each other thinking they would go away if we rolled in close enough to each other."

I continue crying and feeling like I want to disappear. I want to disappear and hide because my therapist probably doesn't think that this was abuse. It's not like he was my father or something. It's not like he tied me up and made me do it. I don't think it was abuse.

I look at her. I continue.

"We just kept rolling into the center of the bed and it went on forever. It went on and on. One would touch us and we would roll and then one would touch us again and we would roll. Then one would try to pull down our pants and we would roll. It just kept going on and on and on.

"Until finally it seemed quiet and we got out of the bed and went into the closet and each of us put on like three pairs of pants and three shirts and like two belts each. For some reason yelling at them was out of the question.

"But I remember feeling so scared and angry and wanting to punch them and get them to leave us the fuck alone. I just wanted to scream, scream as loud as I could. But Jessica and I were both afraid that we'd get into trouble. That's the only reason that I can think of why we didn't scream.

"Eva, I don't understand why I just took it. Why I didn't do something. Why did I just lie there and not get up and scream? That's why it doesn't feel like abuse. I feel that, especially when I was younger, I looked forward to it. I looked forward to it because he was nice to me. He was nice to me and he didn't hit me and he gave me attention.

"GOD, THAT'S SOOOOOOO PATHETIC! I FEEL FUCKING DISGUST-ING!!! I actually looked forward to going there in the summer when I was little because he made me feel special and good and pretty and important. And he wasn't that much older than me. It wasn't like he was my dad."

I stop and look at her.

She has a kind, loving look in her eyes and she speaks.

"Bella, one of your earliest memories was Matt violating you sexually. Did you feel that he was more powerful than you?"

"Of course. He was older and I looked up to him."

"You were a little girl. It doesn't matter if the person who is violating you is older or younger than you. He began violating you sexually at a very young age. And it makes complete sense that you looked forward to it. This is the one place where you weren't afraid of being hit. This is the one place that someone paid attention to you.

"Close your eyes and picture a little girl of five or six. Picture her in your head. Picture her being abused like you were in your home, being afraid and hit and ridiculed and basically tortured by every person in her family.

"Now, do you think that it would be her fault that she craved emotional and physical attention that made her feel visible and important and good?"

"No, of course it wouldn't be her fault. She just wanted to feel important to someone."

For a brief second I start to look at the whole situation a little differently. I start to see that maybe it might not have been all my fault. I continue.

"And when I got older, I didn't like it. I hated it. I wanted to kill him for it."

I stop and think about my grandpa's funeral. And then the brief second is over. It's my fault again. I continue.

"I wanted to kill him but at the same time I would get jealous any time he had a girlfriend. That's so fucked up. It's fucking disgusting. I got fucking jealous of my cousin's fucking girlfriends! And, then when my second cousin Janie came to my grandma's house for the funeral I was devastated."

I take a deep breath and remember.

FLASH!

I'm sitting on the grass at my grandma's and everyone's around. My grandma and uncle and aunt and mom and all of my cousins and my brother. Some are sitting on the porch and us kids are on the grass.

Up pulls this car and this gorgeous girl gets out of the back. She's tall and skinny and tan and absolutely beautiful. I remember it like it was yesterday. She was wearing cut-off jean shorts like Daisy Duke and a tight, white T-shirt.

She could be a model. Easily. She has thin, perfect legs and perfect, big breasts and my heart immediately sinks. I know that I'm going to be invisible for as long as she stays here.

As soon as the adults go inside and it's just us kids outside, my brother and cousin start flirting with her like she's some girl at the swimming pool.

My cousin even says, "Incest is best, put your second cousin to the test," to Janie. I feel so fat and disgusting and unimportant and jealous and insecure. And ashamed.

I go into the house and into my room and cry. It was like my boyfriend had just started flirting with some girl right in front of me. I've never felt so low. I've never felt so incredibly worthless and invisible and disgustingly fat and repulsive. I lie there and think about how I wish I was her. I just wish that I was her.

My aunt comes into the bedroom to see what's wrong with me. That's how fucking oblivious my mom is to anything going on with me. She didn't even come in to see what was wrong. My aunt comes in instead and asks me what is wrong and all I can do is tell her how fat and repulsive and ugly I feel.

She takes me into the bathroom and tells me how pretty and sweet I am. She curls my hair and does my makeup . . .

I stop. I stop and cry. I stop and cry because that is one of the few memories I have of someone in my family taking time to make me feel good. But then I remember how jealous I was and I start to feel shame.

I look at Eva.

"I was fifteen years old and I was jealous of my cousin's attraction to my other cousin. That's fucking disgusting and fucked up and wrong."

She speaks.

"It's not wrong, Bella. It's completely understandable and appropriate behavior. He is someone who, throughout the whole time you were growing up, showed you affection when it suited his needs. And then when someone else came into the picture and caught his eye, you were invisible. Just like your mother. Both of them used you for what they needed and as soon as someone else caught their eyes, you no longer existed."

I look at her. I look at her and cry. I cry and cry and cry for all that I lost. For all that was taken from me. For all that I've had to face in my adulthood because of this. For all of the energy that I used taking my anger out on myself. For all of the energy that I still waste taking my anger out on myself.

For all of the work to come.

TEN YEARS OLD

I look under the pool table across from me and I see Kim. She's naked from her waist up and has only underwear on from the waist down. She's sitting cross-legged and covering her top.

I look to my right side and I see Jen. She's also naked from the waist up and has only underwear on her bottom. She's sitting cross-legged and is covering her top.

There's hooting and hollering. There are boys and girls everywhere. They're all surrounding the pool table.

There's loud music. Some kind of pop music. It's loud because it's a birthday party.

Kim's parents are upstairs and all of us kids are downstairs. We're playing games for the party. We're playing pool.

Strip pool.

But the only people who are naked are me and Jen and Kim. All the other girls don't want to play because they're afraid to get naked.

I'm not afraid. I want them to see me naked. I secretly wish that every time the boys take their shots, they'll make them, and then we'll have to take off more clothes. I want the boys to see me naked because then they will want me and I want them to want me.

The boys are fully dressed. They have taken off only their socks and shoes. The rest of their clothes are on. Not like ours. Ours are in a pile next to the pool table. Ours are in a pile because we are losing.

But we aren't really losing because the boys are getting to see us naked and that's what matters.

There's loud music and shouting and hollering and we are squatting under the table and the boys like it. The girls just kind of watch. But I don't care about the girls.

My attention is on the boys seeing me naked. Because then they will like me and that's what matters. The boys will see me naked and then they'll like me. The boys will like me. They'll think that I'm pretty and that means they like me.

I hear boys hooting and hollering. Not too loud, though, because then Kim's parents will hear.

I hear one boy tell us, "You girls are in trouble now. One more shot and you're naked. You can't cover your tops *and* your bottoms."

Other boys cheer. They cheer because they want to see us naked. *Us!* They want to see us because we're pretty. They want to see us because they want us as girlfriends. They want to see us because we're the popular girls. They want to see us because we're special.

Last shot. He makes it.

We have to get naked. I can feel my heart racing. My heart is racing like it does when I'm scared. It's racing like it does when I think about sledding down a hill at top speed on a tube. It races like it does before Matt does things to me.

I'm ready to take off my underwear. There's cheering all around me. Boys cheer because they want to see me take off my clothes. Boys cheer because they like me. Boys cheer because I'm popular and boys like popular girls to take off their clothes.

"TAKE IT OFF! YOU GIRLS HAVE TO TAKE IT OFF NOW!"

"YEEAAAAH! WOOOO! WOOOO-HOOOOOOO!"

"TAKE IT ALL OFF!!!"

Hollering and shouting and cheering. Loud and louder and louder.

The louder they get the more we know they want us.

We look at each other under the table and decide that it's now or never. Jen and Kim look a little nervous but we decide that it's time. It's time to take it all off for the boys.

As the three of us stand up to take it all off, the music shuts off. The music shuts off and everyone in the place stops smiling and stops hollering.

We turn around, and there stands Kim's dad.

FIFTEEN YEARS OLD

I can't wait for her to get home. She's going to love this. This is the best Mother's Day present ever. Man, she's going to love this. I can't wait to see her face when she sees all of this.

I take another balloon out of the package. I blow and blow and blow until I have absolutely no air left. Until my head is spinning. Until I feel tingly in my face. Until I feel tingly all over. That's a good feeling. I could do this all night long. It's like I'm high but I'm not. It's like it felt at Kelly's birthday party and we all purposely hyperventilated until we passed out. That tingly, high feeling. Good. High. Tingly. Good. Better. Best.

I blow another and another. One after the other and the package is becoming empty.

I keep blowing and tingling. My fingers and face are tingling. My nose is tingling and my fingertips are tingling. I'm blowing and tingling. Blowing and tingling.

I look around our shoebox of a house and see that the brown carpet and the brown kitchen linoleum are starting to become red.

Red. Red with balloons. Red with blowing. Red with love. Red with the excitement that I can't wait to see on her face when she sees all the work that I've put into her Mother's Day. There's a sea of red taking over the living room. I feel happy. I feel excited. I feel so excited to make her feel good.

Every holiday—and other times too—I try to do something really exciting and special to make her feel good. I make her something. I write her something. I cook her something. I read her something. I draw her something. Sometimes I make jewelry. Sometimes I make funny cards with pictures. Sometimes I wake up early and bring her breakfast in bed.

I never buy anything because I don't have money and it doesn't mean as much.

But every holiday I wish that she would be more excited about what I make for her. I guess sometimes it just doesn't feel like I give her enough. Her boyfriends always get her really nice stuff. One year Daryl bought her more than a thousand dollars worth of skiing gear. She paraded around the house jumping for joy, trying everything on, and barely even said thank you to me for my gift.

Sometimes I wish that she would do that with me. I want to see her eyes light up like they do when she gets something from one of them. I wish her eyes would light up for me. I wish that I could make her eyes light up too. I wish and hope and try.

I look around the room. The balloons are all finished and I can't see the floor at all. There's just a sea of red love. Red hope. Red bulbs of excitement. Red. Red. Red.

Red because I love her and she's my mom. Red because red means love and when she sees the red and the love then her eyes will light up for me. Red hope. I hope and hope that she'll feel the love that I put into this and show me the same love back.

I hear her truck pull up. I scan the room to make sure that everything is in place.

The house is spotless. I swept, vacuumed, mopped, dusted, cleaned the bathroom, did the dishes, fed the dogs, did all of the laundry . . . of course, I do those things all the time anyway. But this time I spent twice as long.

I hear the door of the truck shut and I hide behind the front door so that I can surprise her when she comes in.

I hear footsteps. She's coming onto the porch.

I'm so excited. My heart is racing. Pounding. Thumping. Blood is rushing from my arms and legs straight to my head and I'm about to explode with the excitement.

She's going to see the red and the balloons and the love and the time and the effort and the excitement and her eyes are going to light up. Her eyes are going to light up like they do when she gets a present from Daryl. They're going to light up like she loves me more than anyone else in the world. They're going to light up like no one else exists. They're going to light up like I'm the most important person in the world to her. They're going to light up and fill me up.

The door handle turns. The door opens.

"HAPPY MOTHER'S DAY!"

I jump out from behind the door and grab her to give her a kiss and a hug.

"ARABELLA! YOU SCARED ME!"

"I'm sorry Mom. Look at all the balloons. Happy Mother's Day! What do you think?"

"Well, give me a minute. My arms are full of stuff. I need to go change out of these clothes."

She scans the room as she walks to her room.

With a faint smile she says, "This is nice, Arabella. Thank you."

She looks at me with the same look she gives me when I show her that I got an A in school. Or the same look that she gives me any other day that she comes home from work. And she shuts her bedroom door.

Her eyes don't light up. They're dull. No light. None. None at all.

She doesn't see the red. She doesn't see the love. She doesn't see the effort. She doesn't see the time. She doesn't see the extra time that I put into her special day. She doesn't see me. She doesn't see me. She doesn't see me.

It was a dumb, fucking idea.

A dumb, fucking idea to fill the house with balloons.

FIFTEEN YEARS OLD

I take a deep breath. I'm in my room. My mom and Daryl are in the kitchen. My mom insisted on being on the other phone.

I dial. Slowly.

One number. Two. Three. Four.

I take deep breaths. This is the call I've been waiting for my whole life.

Breathe.

This is the call I have needed for my whole life.

Breathe.

My whole life.

Breathe.

All my life.

Breathe.

This is it.

Breathe.

"Okay, Arabella. This is it."

Breathe.

Okay. I can do this. I can do this. I can do this. This is what I have wanted my whole life.

Five. Six. Seven. Eight.

Slower. I dial slower as I get closer to the last numbers. And I breathe. I breathe deep and fast and fast and deep.

Nine. Ten.

BIG BREATH.

Eleven.

The ringing starts. I don't know what I'm going to say. I should just introduce myself. No, I should ask him if he knows an Arabella. I should just say, "I am Arabella." I should just let him ask me questions. I don't know what to say. I can't believe that I'm finally going to talk to him. This is the phone call that I've been waiting for my whole life.

Breathe.

Ring.

Breathe.

Ring.

Inhale. Exhale.

Ring.

Inhale exhale inhale exhale.

Ring.

Inhaleexhaleinhaleexhaleinhaleexhale.

"Hello?"

I can do this. I can do this. I can do this. Breathe, Arabella. Say your name. Say something. Say hello. BREATHE!

"Hello?"

He sounds annoyed now.

"Um, hello. Is this Geoffrey Granovich?"

Yeah, who is this?

"This is Arabella."

Pause. Silence. He doesn't know me. I should hang up. Hang up now. Hang up. He doesn't know me and I should just hang up.

"Umm . . . this is Arabella . . . uh, your, umm, daughter."

"Oh. Huh . . . hi. Huh . . . uh, how are, uh, you?"

"I'm fine. I'm good. How are you?"

"I'm . . . uh . . . good."

"Is it okay that I'm calling you?"

"Uh . . . um, yeah."

Silence. Silence. Deafening silence. Deafening. Silence.

"So, uh, Arabella, what grade are you in?"

"I'm in tenth grade."

"Oh, that's good. So . . . that would make you how old?"

"I'm fifteen. All the other kids are sixteen. But my birthday's in August so I don't turn sixteen until the school year is over."

Silence. Silence. This is the weirdest conversation I think I've ever had. This is so uncomfortable. Totally uncomfortable. Fucking uncomfortable.

"Do you have any pets?"

"Yeah, we have shepherds. A black one named Scooter and a brown one named Joker. They're great."

"Oh . . . well, that's nice."

"Do you have any dogs, Geoff?"

"Uh . . . no."

Silence. Silence. Uncomfortable silence. I don't know what the fuck to think but I know that I need to ask him if I can come see him.

He speaks again.

"Do you have a boyfriend?"

I giggle. An uncomfortable giggle. I'm uncomfortable that he wants to know if I have a boyfriend.

"No, not right now."

Silence. Silence again. Silence with discomfort. Discomfort that could be sliced with a butcher knife. It's now or never. Just ask him. Just do it. It's now or never. Now or never.

I take a deep, uncomfortable, shaky, insecure breath and I ask him.

"Geoff?"

"Yeah?"

"I was wondering if I could, um . . . well, come out and see you sometime?"

Silence. Silence. Silence. Suspenseful silence. I sit and hope and wait in suspense. My heart pounds and I sit in the suspenseful discomfort. Waiting. Waiting. Waiting.

He speaks.

"Well, uh, yeah. I guess that would be okay. When?"

"I was thinking this summer."

"Uh, okay."

I am elated. Ecstatic. Jumping for joy. I can't contain myself. My dad wants to meet me. My real dad is going to let me come see him. I'm going to meet my real dad! My real dad! My real fucking dad!

"Uh, Arabella, I need to talk to your mom alone for a minute. I'll talk to you later, okay?"

"Yeah, sure. No problem, Geoff."

I don't care that he wants to talk to my mom. I got the answer that I wanted. He probably just wants to talk about when I get to go see him. About how long I'll stay for. About what kind of clothes I should bring.

I lie on my bed and stare at the ceiling and smile. I smile and my stomach swirls and jumps for joy. I'm going to meet my real fucking dad. I can't believe it. I can't believe I just talked to my real dad.

I am happier than I've ever felt in my whole life. My whole fucking life.

I hear a knock on the door.

Through the door my mom says, "Arabella, can you come out here for a second?"

"Sure! I'm coming!"

I jump up out of my bed and skip down the hall and into the kitchen with a smile on my face the whole way there. Until I see my mom and Daryl.

"Arabella, sit down for a minute, okay?"

"What, Mom? What's wrong?"

"Daryl and I need to tell you something that is probably going to hurt your feelings but that you need to hear."

I look at her and I look at Daryl. I look back at her.

"What, Mom? Is it about Geoff? Is he okay?"

"He's fine. But I need to tell you what he said when you got off of the phone with him, okay?"

I look at Daryl. He looks like he knows I'm about to get punched in the stomach. He looks like he knows I'm about to walk a plank. He looks at me like I've never seen him look at me.

"Arabella, I'm just going to come out and say it. This is the reason that I didn't think that it was a good idea for you to contact him."

I start to feel RAGE. How dare she start to bash him again! That's all she's ever done. Bash him. How abusive he was. What a drunk he was. How he abandoned us. How he didn't love us. How he cheated on her when she was pregnant. How he skipped the state so that he could hide and not have to pay child support. How he would only allow Bill to adopt us if he was released from paying all the back child support he owed. How he was a big fucking loser.

She starts again.

"This is going to be hard for you to hear, but I have to tell you what he said."

She takes a breath and looks at Daryl and looks back at me.

"He said that he didn't want you to come visit. He said that he—and these were his exact words—he doesn't want to open this book."

I stare at her. I stare at her with hatred. I want to punch her in the face. I want to smack the fucking lies out of her. I want to hurt her. Hurt and punch and smack.

Daryl speaks.

"Arabella, this is true. I was right here when he said it."

I look at her and then I look at Daryl.

"BULLSHIT! YOU TWO ARE FUCKING LIARS! YOU JUST DON'T WANT ME TO SEE HIM BECAUSE YOU DON'T LIKE HIM. YOU THINK BECAUSE HE DOESN'T

LOVE YOU THEN HE SHOULDN'T LOVE ME EITHER! YOU'RE FUCKING SELFISH LIARS!"

Tears are searing down my face. Sizzling and scalding as they roll over the RAGEful heat of my cheeks.

I run to my room and slam the door and cry and wait for him to call me. I cry and rage. I rage at my mom's lies. I want to smack her. I want to punch her. I want to beat the fucking hell out of her. I want to beat the lies out of her.

I fucking hate her. I fucking hate her. I fucking hate her.

She just wants to keep me away from him and she'll do anything she can.

I cry and I wait for his call. I cry until my pillow is soaked. I wait for his call and cry and cry and cry.

But his call never comes.

Ever.

TWENTY-NINE YEARS OLD

(Day One, 4:28 p.m.)

As I pace around the house all I can think of is how this happened. Maybe *it's* not what I think *it* is. Maybe this and maybe that.

I bounce back and forth from Rage to denial to excruciating pain and bewilderment.

SMACK!

I found *it*.

SMACK!

It's his.

SMACK! SMACK!

It's his and he's been lying to me.

SMACK!

Maybe *it's* not his. Maybe *it's* someone else's.

I pace. Pace and pace and pace. I'm practically running around the house. Running and dodging. Dodging balls of pain. Dodging balls of belief. Dodging balls of reality.

I'm frantic. Panicky. Urgent. I feel like I just snorted a huge line of crank. I need to get out and go and run and never come back. Run and find something. Anything to make this all go away. Anything. Just go and run.

Two cars pull up in the driveway. My friends are here. I have to tell them. No, I have to entertain them. Maybe I shouldn't tell them. No, I have to. No, I can't.

DING DONG.

I open the door and when I see Heather's face I start to bawl. I start to sob. I can't hold it back as hard as I try. The balls have finally hit me. I can't dodge anymore. I am defeated.

I open my mouth to ask her how she is and instead I blurt out, "I was looking for matches. I was looking for matches and I don't know what came over me. Something told me to keep looking around and I did. I saw this box in his closet and something told me to look inside. And when I did I found all of this stuff."

I point to the table where the *its* are sitting.

As I point and show her and wait for her shock and amazement to form into words, the rest of the girls arrive.

We're all standing in the kitchen looking at the table. The table full of *its*. I'm sobbing and crying. And shocking. And denying. And bewildering. And in a completely different reality.

They're all wonderful to me. They're all wonderful and try to help me figure out what to do. My feelings. My plan. They ask if I have talked to him. I say that I called him and he wasn't there. I left a message. I didn't tell him what about. I just asked him to call me.

As I stand there I can't believe this is happening to me. This can't be happening. I tell them that this can't be happening. Nothing feels real. I feel like I'm in a dream. A fucking nightmare.

I show Carnie his computer. I show her that there's a password on it. There's a password. Why does he need a password unless he's hiding something else from me? I don't get it? Why? Why? WHY?!?!?!

As we talk I hear the song "Unchained Melody" begin to play. That's him. That's his ring. I pull myself together and pick up the phone. As I do the Rage starts to grow inside.

RAGE. Contempt. Anger. Seething. Doubt. Denial. RAGE! RAGE! RAGE!

I say, "Hello?"

"Hey, kid. What's up?"

"I found your shit."

Silence. Dead fucking silence. Guilty fucking silence. The kind of silence that occurs when someone is shocked and surprised and is trying to come up with a lie to cover his ass.

The RAGE grows. Swirling around in my stomach. Twisting and contorting every cell and organ in my body. My hair starts to ache. I tremble. RAGING tremble. Seething tremble. Betrayal tremble. The tremble of reality hitting me.

"What shit?"

"What fucking shit? Are you fucking kidding me? You know what fucking shit I'm talking about."

"No. I don't."

I'm enraged now. I'm dealing with a scolded child who will do anything to avoid the consequences. A hurricane has taken over my body. Over my whole body. I am swirling and twisting and contorting and changing into something else. Everything in me is now someone else. I don't know this person and I never have. I have never seen this person before. Him or Me.

"DON'T FUCKING LIE TO ME, STEVE! I'M NOT FUCKING STUPID, OKAY? THE SHIT IN YOUR FUCKING CLOSET, IN YOUR GOD-DAMN TOOL BOX! SERIOUSLY! DO YOU THINK THAT I'M GOING TO BELIEVE THAT YOU DON'T KNOW WHAT THE FUCK I'M TALKING ABOUT, THAT YOU DON'T KNOW WHAT THE FUCK IS

IN YOUR OWN BEDROOM CLOSET? JESUS FUCKING CHRIST. GIVE ME A FUCKING BREAK! I OPENED THE BOX AND FOUND *IT!!*"

No more tears. Simply RAGE. Fury. Wrath. Thunder and eruption. I want to explode. I want to smack him. I want to rip the fucking truth out of his heart.

I want the dignity I fucking deserve.

"WELL? WHAT THE FUCK, STEVE? ARE YOU GONNA FESS UP?"

Pause.

"*It's* not mine. *It's* Jon's. I'm holding *it* for him."

SMACK!

Cool, calm, and collected. He says it like he would if he were to tell me that the sky is grey today. He says it as if there's no doubt in his mind. He says it as though he fucking believes it. He says it as if he thinks *I* will believe it. He's lying through his teeth and there's no nervousness. No doubt. Just pure matter-of-fact confidence. Unfuckingbelievable!

"YOU CAN'T BE FUCKING SERIOUS! ARE YOU FUCKING SERIOUS? WHO DOES JON NEED TO HIDE THE SHIT FROM ANYWAY? YOU EXPECT ME TO BELIEVE THAT HE NEEDS TO HIDE HIS SHIT IN YOUR CLOSET? DO YOU THINK I'M FUCKING STUPID? AND WHY THE HELL DO YOU HAVE A PASSWORD ON YOUR COMPUTER? WHAT THE HELL ARE YOU TRYING TO HIDE FROM ME? THERE'S A LOT YOU'RE NOT TELLING ME AND I WANT TO FUCKING KNOW. NOW! I NEED YOU TO COME HOME RIGHT NOW. WE NEED TO FUCKING TALK AND YOU NEED TO FUCKING TELL ME THE TRUTH!!!"

Pause.

Longer pause.

"Okay. I'll be there in about an hour."

TWENTY-SEVEN YEARS OLD

I lie in his arms. I lie in the nook. My head is in his nook, the nook of his chest and the nook of his shoulder. I stare at the hairs on his chest and feel the soft warmth of his skin on my face. I feel the softness and warmth and melt into his embrace.

I'm warm and comfortable and safe like I have never felt before. Never in my life have I felt this connected to someone. Never in my life have I been able to make love to someone without thinking about other people. Never in my life have I felt beautiful and free and unconcerned with the fat on my thighs or the shape of my breasts or the many other flaws that I've worried about with every other lover that I've had.

Never in my life have I trusted anyone like this. Never, ever have I felt like I am number one to someone. Never, ever have I felt completely and totally accepted for who I am.

As I feel the warmth and enjoy the candlelight reflecting off of the ceiling and on his skin, I make little circles on his chest with my finger tip. I trace hearts and squares and circles and hearts and hearts and hearts.

I smell his skin. I smell the sweet remnants of his sweat. I smell the remains of his cologne. I smell the intimacy and gentleness and connection that we had while making love just now. I smell the love that he feels for me. I smell his love. There's no other smell like it.

As I lie naked, tracing the shapes and smelling his love, I start to feel scared. I start to feel scared that he's going to leave me. Leave me like my mom left me. Leave me like my dad left me. I start to feel scared that he'll hurt me. I start to feel scared that he'll use me. I start to feel scared that he's like every other person in my life that was close to me.

FLASH!

My mom and I are on the phone. I ask her to sign a piece of paper so that I can get my medical history from the adoption services. I ask her because I have pre-cancerous cells and I need to know my history.

She tells me that she doesn't want to send away for her adoption information. She has no interest in finding out where she came from.

I tell her that she doesn't have to be involved. I just need her to sign a piece of paper so that I can get the forms released to me. I need to know my history. She doesn't have to be involved. I just need it. I need it for me. She doesn't have to be involved.

She starts to get angry and tells me she doesn't want to be involved. She tells me I'm selfish. It stings.

Now I'm angry. I'm angry because she's acting like a child who has to get her way and I'm angry because there's no reason for her not to do this. No reason except for her need to have control.

It's always the same with her. Like when I was growing up. I would ask her if I could spend the night at a friend's house and she'd tell me no for absolutely no reason. I would ask her why and she'd tell me, "Because I said so, that's why."

She just likes to deny me. I don't know why, but I truly believe that she gets something out of denying me.

I tell her that I really need my medical history, that it's okay that she doesn't want to find out about her birth parents. She doesn't have to, because all she has to do is sign a piece of paper. That's it. That's all she has to do. "Please," I beg her, "please do this." I tell her that this isn't about her. This is about me. I tell her that she's the one being selfish.

"I SAID NO! PEOPLE GET SICK AND DIE, ARABELLA! DEAL WITH IT!"

She hangs up . . .

That was four months ago. I haven't spoken to her since. She is the master of disappearing from my life. Disappearing because I'm mean and selfish and not worthy of her love. Disappearing because I am nothing to her. Disappearing because I don't fill her the way that I used to. Disappearing because I want to be mothered by her. Disappearing because she can't stand me. Disappearing because I won't put up with her shit anymore. Disappearing because that's what she does best.

As I lie in his arms and smell his skin and feel his nakedness he looks down at me and asks me why I'm crying. He says it with a sincerity I've never heard from anyone who's been this close to me. He says it with complete compassion and love.

I hadn't even realized that I was crying. I was in the other world. The world where my mother doesn't love me. The world where no one loves me. The world that I grew up in. The world of not feeling love. The world where I am not good enough. The world where my needs come last. The world where my needs don't come at all. The world where all I feel is need. The world where I am nothing.

I sob in his arms. I sob and tell him how afraid I am that he'll leave me. I sob and tell him that I'm afraid that he'll hurt me. I sob and tell him that I've never known anyone who was close to me that didn't use, abuse, or neglect me. I sob and tell him that I can't believe that he won't do the same. I can't believe he won't do the same because I feel like I am nothing.

I sob and sob and sob. My tears create a warm puddle on his chest. He holds me and caresses my back and plays with my hair.

He rolls out from under me and places himself half on top of me and half on the bed. He gently raises my chin with his hand. He draws my eyes up to his. He draws my eyes up to his and he looks at me with the tenderness of an angel. He strokes my hair with one hand and he speaks.

"I will never hurt you. I will never hurt you because I love you. You are the most amazing woman that I have ever met. I am never going anywhere. You hear me? Never. The only way I'm leaving is if you get rid of me."

He continues with his gaze of adoration and strokes of my hair and tender caresses on my skin.

"I will never leave you because you are the most loving woman I know.

"I will never leave you because despite the horrors that you grew up in, you are the most selfless person I know.

"I will never leave you because you are the most intelligent woman I know.

"I will never leave you because you carry a passion for life that is unsurpassed by any person I know.

"I will never leave you because you care for your animals with the love and tenderness that a mother would for her child.

"I will never leave you because you believe in the goodness of all people.

"I will never leave you because you are the strongest and most courageous person I've ever met.

"I will never leave you because your smile lights up every room you walk into.

"I will never leave you because you have an energy that makes people want to be around you.

"An energy that makes people believe in themselves and everything they want to accomplish.

"An energy that makes people feel better about themselves as they walk away from you.

"I will never leave you because when I look into your eyes I know that you really see me.

"I will never leave you because when I am around you I want to be a better person.

"I will never leave you because I am a better person because of you.

"I will never leave you because I look at the world differently because I know you.

"I will never leave you because you see the world the way things should be and you're doing something about it.

"I will never leave you because you have changed who I am.

"I will never leave you because you are my heart.

"I will never leave you because you are different from other people.

"I will never leave you because there is something that sets you apart from the rest of the people in the world.

"Bella, I will never leave you because you are a miracle."

I feel warm. I feel more loved by him than I have ever felt in my life. I feel complete.

I look into his eyes and say, "Thank you, Steve."

I look into his eyes and think, I'm going to spend my life with this man.

TWENTY-FIVE YEARS OLD

I raise my hand and wait for the professor to call on me. I've got to say something about this. I have to. Even if it is politically incorrect. I have to say it because it has to be said.

She calls on me.

I speak.

"I think that there's a point at which respecting a culture must take a backseat to paying attention to human rights."

She responds.

"Yes, but that's based on *your* cultural beliefs. Do you think that it's really fair to say that the ways by which another culture raises their children are wrong because their way isn't the way that you would do it? Isn't it fair to say that you think that your way is the right way, because your culture has taught you that way? And would you want someone from another culture to look at the way that you do things and say that your way is the wrong way because it isn't their way?"

I feel flustered and bombarded. Words escape me and I've lost my train of thought. Everyone is staring at me and judging me. Staring at me and judging me. They all think I'm fucking stupid. An idiot. They're all thinking bad things about me. They think I'm dumb and they think that I should shut up.

I want to say, Well, first of all, I believe that if someone came along and told me that their way was the right way to raise a child, I would ask them to show me why and how. If I believed that it was of value to the child's wellbeing, I would want to learn more about it. And if the person could show me that it was a better way, I'd be all for it.

I also want to say, Second of all, I don't think that my way is the right way just because my culture taught me how it should be. I believe what I believe because I grew up in a really violent and scary house—that's where I learned what wasn't okay. My culture didn't teach me that. My culture says it's okay to spank. I don't agree. I don't think that corporal punishment is good for the wellbeing of a child. And many experts in that area of study would agree.

I want to say, Third, I think that there are certain behaviors that are totally unacceptable and I don't care what culture one is from. That doesn't matter to me. It is not okay when little girls are sold into sexual slavery because a family member committed a crime. Some behaviors are simply never okay. Period. Culture doesn't matter when it comes to the wellbeing of children. I will not tolerate or respect this sort of behavior simply because it's politically correct to respect another's cultural differences.

But I don't say any of this. I'm too flustered and tongue-tied and stupid. There are too many eyes on me. Too many judgments. Too many people thinking about how fucking dumb I am.

I can hear their voices in their heads.

"God, she's a fucking idiot."

"She's a fucking moron."

"She's fucking stupid."

"She is fucking ridiculous."

"God, I'm glad I'm not as obnoxious as she is."

I can hear their voices ridiculing me and berating me and condemning me. They berate, ridicule, and condemn.

I can see their eyes telling me that I should shut the fuck-up. Telling me that I'm annoying. Telling me that I'm stupid, a fucking stupid, obnoxious girl who should just shut up. Telling me I'm stupid. Dumb. Idiot. Bitch. Brainless. Laughable. Asinine.

And so instead I say, "I just think it's wrong."

NINETEEN YEARS OLD

"I can't believe Ramie's parents are dead. I just can't believe it, Mom. They were my home away from home when you and Bill were together. I can't believe it."

She looks at me with that look that she gets whenever she's been drinking. Like she's confused. That stupid fucking look. That stupid fucking look that she gets. Her eyes get buggy and unfocused. They get huge. Her face tightens. She tries to look serious. But she just ends up looking drunk and stupid.

I swirl the cheap wine around in my glass and know that I don't look like her when I've been drinking. I look in the mirror as I sit on the bathroom countertop. I look nothing like that. I look like me, only with red eyes. Red eyes and fat fucking thighs.

I stare into the mirror and look into my red eyes and think about my fat fucking thighs. I look nothing like her and I am nothing like her. I'm huge and fat and she's skinny and petite. I look nothing like her and I am nothing like her. I look nothing like her and I am nothing like her. I look noth—

"Arabella, I have to tell you something."

I look at her and her stupid, bug-eyed expression. Her stupid bug-eyes, and her face is trying to look more serious than usual. And so she looks more stupid than usual. Oh fuck; what is she going to fucking tell me now? Can't wait to hear this.

"What?"

"Well, if I tell you, you have to promise not to tell anyone, okay?"

"What, Mom? Just tell me."

I'm annoyed now. I'm annoyed because she's drunk. I'm annoyed because she has that stupid, fucking bug-eyed look. I'm annoyed because she's trying to be serious while she sways back and forth with her bug eyes. She's such a fucking child.

She manages to sit down on the toilet and she gets comfortable. As comfortable as she can swaying back and forth.

She looks me in the eyes again and with her most seriously stupid expression says, "Promise me that you won't tell anyone."

"Okay, okay. I promise."

"Swear, Arabella. I want you to swear that you won't tell anyone."

"Okay, I fucking swear. Now tell me what you were going to tell me already."

She sits. She takes a drunken breath in and sways. She sways and sits and breathes in her wine breath and looks fucking stupid. She looks like a fucking frog. A fucking frog with huge drunk eyes and a tight neck and she just looks like a goddamn fucking frog.

She takes a swig of her cheap wine. She sits and sways and stares at the counter. So I take a swig of my cheap wine.

"Mom, I'm starting to get annoyed. Will you just tell me what you were going to tell me already?"

She takes another drunken breath and starts to tell me.

"Remember back when Bill and I had just gotten separated?"

"Yeah, I remember."

"Remember how Ramie always used to spend the night?"

"Yeaaaaah. And?"

I don't know what she's about to tell me but I'm starting to get fucking worried. I'm starting to get worried because she's bringing up Ramie. This is not fucking good. Not fucking good at all.

She continues.

"Well, do you remember how I used to date a lot? Like when I brought that one guy, Davell, home. Remember you and Dave used to call him Devil?"

"Yeah, I remember. What the hell does Ramie have to do with this, Mom?"

I'm starting to get impatient. My mom and her stupid fucking bug eyes. Her fucking frog eyes. Get to the fucking point already. It's always the same with her. She takes ten minutes to do something that would take a normal person one minute. She takes an hour telling a story that takes five minutes to tell. Hurry the fuck-up already. Jesus fucking Christ! You bring up my best friend and tell me that I need to promise not to fucking tell anyone. What the fuck! JUST FUCKING TELL ME ALREADY!

"I'm getting there. Just hold on, Bella."

She takes another drunken, swaying breath.

"Well, did Ramie ever tell you that she saw anything during that time? The time after Bill was gone and I was dating."

The RAGE is growing. I want to smack the fucking words from her mouth. I want to shake her until they come tumbling onto the counter. I want to smack her stupid fucking frog face off.

"MOM, WHAT THE FUCK ARE YOU TALKING ABOUT? NO! NO, SHE NEVER TOLD ME ANYTHING WEIRD. SPIT OUT WHAT YOU'RE TALKING ABOUT. PLEASE, MOM!"

Now she looks scared of me. She's got that stupid, pathetic-little-child look she gets when I tell her she's done something wrong to me or when I'm upset with her. It makes me sick. It makes me want to smack her. It makes me feel RAGE. It makes me feel sorry for her.

She starts again, with her pathetic, wounded child expression.

"Well, one night I came home from the bar."

"Yeah? What else?"

"Well, I did something that I would never do now. I would never do it now. I don't know why I did it."

"WHAT, MOM? JUST SPIT IT OUT ALREADY!!!!"

I have no patience for her beating around the fucking bush right now. I have no fucking patience for her stupid feel-fucking-sorry-for-me act. I have no fucking patience at all. I just want to hear the fucking truth. Jesus, what the fuck is she going to say?!?!

She goes on.

"Well . . . I was really drunk and brought these two guys home with me."

Oh my God! My fucking mom is a goddamn whore. A fucking whore. Holy shit. I can't fucking believe this. I can't fucking believe this. My heart starts to race and I start to feel scared. My heart is pounding and racing and scaring me. Ramie?!?! What the fuck does Ramie have to do with this story? Fuck, Fuck, Fuck.

"I was so drunk that we started to mess around in the living room."

"WHAT DO YOU MEAN 'MESS AROUND?' AND WHY IN THE LIVING ROOM AND NOT YOUR ROOM?"

"Well . . . we . . . uh . . . started to get naked. We started to get naked and they were both doing things to me and we didn't go into the bedroom because I didn't want to wake you and Ramie up. Your room was right on the other side of mine and I didn't want to expose you to any of that."

I laugh. A laugh that says, You're fucking unbelievable. A laugh that says, You've got to be fucking kidding me! A laugh that says, You're actually trying to tell me that you were thinking of my best fucking interest by staying in the living room while you got fucked by two guys you brought home from the bar while your daughter and her best fucking friend were sleeping less than twenty-five feet away?!?!?!?! HA! A laugh that says, Give me a fucking break!

I stare at her with disgust. Utter fucking disgust and repulsion and embarrassment and shock.

"I swear, Arabella, I was thinking of you."

She starts to sniffle and her fucking frog eyes start to well with tears of manipulation. Her tears aren't tears of pain. They're tears of manipulation. They used to get me to feel sorry for her. I've seen these tears many, many times and she always uses them when she needs me to feel sorry for her. They go hand in hand with the pathetic-little-child look.

"Mom, just fucking tell me what you have to tell me. Seriously."

"Well . . . in the middle of them . . . um . . . doing what they were doing, I heard the bedroom door open. Ramie walked out and saw us."

"WHAT?!?!?!?!? WHAT THE FUCK DID SHE DO?"

"She just turned around and went back into the bedroom. I think she was going to get a drink of water. I don't think she even knew what was going on. I think she was half asleep and doesn't remember."

I shake my head. Trying to shake off what I just heard. It doesn't work. I take a swig of my cheap-ass wine and shake my head again. I shake it over and over.

I try to shake off the vision of Ramie walking out of the bedroom to find my mom with two men fucking her.

I try to shake off the idea that my best friend saw my mom getting fucked by two fucking slime balls that she brought home from the bar.

I try to shake off my mom never telling me this until now.

I try to shake off my best friend never telling me this.

I try to shake off the memories of my best friend acting weird around my mom after her divorce from Bill.

I try to shake off the fact that my mom's a big fucking slut.

I try to shake off the shame. I try to shake off the horror.

And I try to shake off the disgraceful reality that I came from this woman.

I try, but it does no good.

So I go to find the cheap-ass bottle of wine.

ELEVEN YEARS OLD

I step up the three steps of the school bus and look for him. I look in the back because his bus stop is the first and he gets to sit in the very back. The back is where all the cool people sit. Only the nerds sit up front.

I see him in the back. My heart starts to beat faster. I start to get that quick feeling in my stomach. That quick, excited feeling.

I walk down the aisle and wait for him to wave me to him, or to say hi, or to smile at me. Smile at me to tell me to come and sit by him.

I look at him and walk and wait for his smile. The smile that will let me know that he likes me and wants me to be his girlfriend. The smile that calls me back to sit in his seat with him. The smile that lets me know that he likes me like he did last night.

FLASH!

We hop into the back of the truck. My dad's junkie, green, beat-up truck with the rusty canopy.

We've just gotten out of our confirmation classes at our church. Finally. I can't stand those classes. All we do is talk about the stupid Bible. I can't listen to it. None of it makes any sense. None at all.

It's dark out. It's dark out so no one can see us. We move ourselves up close to the cab of the truck and our backs are against it. We sit close to each other because it's cold in the back of the truck.

My parents give him a ride home from church class because he lives right down the road from me. Our parents trade off. But I like it better when my parents pick us up.

His name is James. James Williamson. I've thought that he was cute since I saw him a year ago when I first moved here in the fourth grade. He was in my class. He's really cute and so is his brother. And he's really popular. And so is his brother.

He scoots a little closer to me as we pull out of the church parking lot.

I think that he likes me. He's really cute and I think he likes me. I think he likes me because of the way he looks at me sometimes . . .

FLASH! FLASH!

I sip my fake cocktail at our make-believe bar in my grandma's basement. Matt winks at me and looks at me with that look like he really likes me. He flirts with me by the way that he looks at me . . .

FLASH!

It's quiet. I stare out the window at the lake as we drive around it. I stare out the window and wish that he could kiss me without my dad seeing. I wish that he could kiss me and then I would feel really good. I think he wants to because of the way that he looks at me. I think that James likes me because of the way that he looks at me like Matt does.

I feel a hand on my leg. I feel his hand on my leg. My heart immediately starts to pound faster and faster and I get that excited feeling in my stomach. I get that excited feeling in my stomach like he likes me and he's going to show me how much.

I look at him and in the dark I see him smiling. A flirty smile. Just like Matt's.

I smile back at him. A flirty smile. A smile that says go ahead, touch me. I want you to touch me. I want you to touch me because you're James and you're cute and popular. And I like you. And I want you to like me.

His hand moves up my leg and in between them. He starts to rub on top of my pants.

My heart beats faster and I get that warm throbby feeling that I get when Matt touches me down there. Throbby and warm and excited and scared. Scared that my dad will see. Scared that he'll make me lose control like Matt does.

He takes his other hand and uses it to help his other one undo the button and zipper on my pants.

My heart races more. My heart pounds and pounds and thuds and thuds faster and faster. The feeling between my legs is warmer and more excited. Warmer and warmer and throbby and throbbier. It's throbby and feels like it's swelling up like a water balloon.

Throb.

He likes me.

Throb.

He really likes me.

Throb-Throb-Throb-Throb.

He really, really likes me.

James is making me throb. Me! ME! He likes Me. James likes ME!

He slides his hands into my pants and he starts to move his fingers around. He starts to move them around and I feel warmer and more excited and more happy and throbby and scared. Scared. Scared. Scared. Scared that Bill will see. Scared that my dad will see James touching me and making me throb.

We turn off the main road and it's pitch dark. There aren't any streetlights on our long and windy road through the hills and the houses.

I feel his breath on my face and his lips hit my face right below my lips. He finds my mouth and he sticks his tongue inside of it. He sticks his tongue in my mouth and he kisses and moves his fingers around in my pants.

Throb. Throb. Throbthrobthrobthrobthrobthrob.

I'm getting that feeling that I get when Matt is licking me down there. That feeling like my body is going to lose control. That feeling feels so good. That feeling makes me want to explode. That feeling is one I know I am not supposed to get when Matt is doing that to me . . .

As the bus starts to move and I walk down the aisle looking for a seat, I wait for James to motion me towards him and I look at him.

SMACK!

He looks at me and then looks away. He doesn't look back at me.

My heart sinks. My stomach starts to feel twisted and sick. I feel tears because I am invisible.

I am invisible. I am invisible. I am invisible.

I sink into my seat and cry.

And disappear.

TWENTY-SEVEN YEARS OLD

I sit on the far end of the couch and ramble on about my mom and how fucked up it was growing up with her.

I tell my therapist about how she used to walk around the house naked. How she always used to walk around naked while she got ready for work. She would stand in the bathroom and put her makeup on and do her hair naked.

I tell her how bothered I was by this. Not so much about the nakedness as much as how she had really big, perfect boobs and I didn't have any. How she had football player legs and a bubble butt and how she told me that I had the same exact body as her except that I was BIGger and less busty.

I start to feel RAGE.

I tell my therapist that I want to punch my mom in the face for telling me how BIG I was. I want to fucking punch her for telling me that what I eat will make me fat. I tell her that I feel like biting my mom's face off. I feel like screaming in her face. I want to fucking scream in her face!

My therapist asks me what I would scream at my mom if she were right here in front of me.

I start. And a flood ensues.

A FLASH FLOOD!

"Why the fuck didn't you ever tell me that you had a boob job? You let me grow up thinking that there was something wrong with me because I didn't have boobs like yours. You let me fucking suffer and hate myself and ask you over and over why my boobs were small and why yours were huge and perky and perfect.

"And then when you did tell me that you had a fucking boob job, you lied about why you got it. You fucking told me that one of your boobs was covered in cysts so you had to get one because it was practically gone compared to the other one. And Grandma told me that was fucking bullshit. She told me that you never had big boobs, that one Christmas you came home to visit and suddenly your boobs were huge.

"You're a fucking liar. You fucking lie about everything. EVERYTHING! You tell people stories that never fucking happened to make yourself look better. And you have no fucking memory of anything bad that happened to me. You only remember when Bill beat *you*. You only called the cops when Bill beat *you*."

I take a breath and RAGE on. My heart beats faster and angrier and it beats on and on in RAGE and fury. The flood continues and my voice rises.

"You fucking compared my body to yours all the fucking time. You basically told me that I was HUGE, when actually I was a fucking rail! You told me that I had thunder thighs and a fucking bubble butt like you, only I was BIGger. You compared me to you in every fucking way!

"I hate how you used to run around the house naked. Run around the house fucking naked in front of me and Dave. Run around the house naked like you were on fucking display or something. You ran around the house naked even when we were in high school. You were totally fucking inappropriate as a fucking mother. Mothers are not supposed to fucking walk around naked in front of their teenage kids. It's fucking sick!

"You never once built *my* fucking self-esteem. I was always the one filling you up. Reassuring you. I can't count how many fucking times I told you that you didn't look old. That you were pretty. That you weren't fat. How many fucking times did you ask me, 'Do I look old? Am I pretty?' Feed me. Feed me. Fucking Feed me.

"That's all I did was feed you. All the time. It was a fucking full-time job. I spent all my energy telling you to leave Bill. How was it that as a fucking eight- or nine-year-old *I* knew that you needed to leave him and you didn't? You would sit in the fucking garage and drink your fucking vodka and ask me what to do. And then you never fucking listened. You never once fucking listened to me!

"When I tried to kill myself you asked my best friend why I would do such a thing. Like you had no fucking clue about why I would possibly want to fucking die. You were a selfish, fucking oblivious mother. But you weren't oblivious. Every summer you purposely sent me to stay at Grandma's, who you knew lived right next to your sexual abuser's house—at whose house I would spend most of my time—just so that you could be alone and have some time to yourself.

"You fucking disappear on me whenever I bring up anything that you should take responsibility for, and I fucking hate you for that. I fucking hate that you spoil Dave even though he's fucked you over and over and over. You can't even call me on a regular basis to see how I'm doing. It's all about you. Fucking you. Marsha. Marsha. Marsha.

"You're a selfish fucking bitch! A fucking narcissistic bitch who was never a fucking mother to me. You sucked me dry and used me and abused me and I fucking hate you."

I stop. I stare at her.

I stop and take a deep breath. I take a deep breath. I breathe in and out and in and out, and as I do my fists unclench and my jaw softens.

And the flood of RAGE stops.

It stops because I can't feel it anymore. It stops because I can't be in that place anymore. It stops because I can't feel the RAGE and the fury and the anger anymore. I can't. I just can't. I don't know how to feel this and really, really feel it. Really, really be in it.

I breathe deep and calm and release and calm again. And I start to cry. Sob. Pain. Grief. Loss. Alone. Alone. Alone.

And the flood of sorrow and guilt begins.

Because sorrow and guilt are easier to navigate.

SIXTEEN YEARS OLD

I roll over and stare at the clock. My head throbs and pounds and I need water. I'm thirsty. Fucking thirsty and I need water because I feel sick and my mouth is dry.

I pull myself out of bed. My head is pounding like it does every time I wake up after a night of hard drinking. I'm thirsty. I'm pounding. My hands are shaking.

Must drink. Must get Advil. Must stop shaking. Shaking and throbbing and aching and thirst. My nose and throat are filled with cotton and I need to drink. If I drink I will feel better.

I walk to the door and with every step my head pounds. Pounds and throbs and aches.

I open my bedroom door and the sound hurts my head. I walk out to the living room. I hear the TV. I'm on a mission to the refrigerator. I need cold water. Cold, icy, thirst-quenching water. Water. Water. Water.

I have no idea how I got home last night or even what I was doing. I just know that I was drinking because of the throbbing and aching and shaking and cotton in my nose and throat. I don't know if I fucked someone or if I threw up in front of people. Neither would be out of the ordinary. Neither would be not remembering. Actually, remembering is more out of the ordinary.

I pound and throb my way down the hall. The fridge seems so far away. I can see it. I'm getting closer. But it feels so far away.

I walk up to it and open it. My muscles ache and throb as I grab the door and pull. It takes every ounce of energy I have to grab it and pull. Grab and pull and ache and throb.

But it's worth it. I reach up for the water jug and unscrew the lid. I put the opening to my mouth. I drink. I drink and drink and drink.

I gulp and gulp and gulp and gulp.

I chug and chug and chug and chug.

All that matters is getting water right now. Nothing else exists, just the coldness and the iciness in my throat. Water, water, water.

I hold onto the jug—and what's left in it—and walk over to the couch and lie down. I lie and throb and ache and pound. I set the jug down next to me and zone out in front of the TV.

Out of the corner of my eye something looks off. I look over and see that the picture is crooked and there's a scrape mark on the wall from the picture sliding across it too hard.

There's glass on the floor. There's glass on the floor and the sconces aren't on the wall beside the picture.

How the hell did that happen? What the fuck?

"MOM, WHAT HAPPENED TO THE WALL?" I call out.

Her bedroom door is shut. I look outside and see that both her and Daryl's trucks are here. So they're in the bedroom.

I call out again.

"MOM, ARE YOU IN THERE?"

The door opens. First she walks out and Daryl is behind her. They look at me like I'm the devil. Seriously.

"YOU CAN'T BE SERIOUS, ARABELLA!"

She looks at me with that look of disgust and annoyance that she gets whenever I'm supposed to know what the fuck she's talking about but don't.

I look at Daryl. He has the look of condemnation.

"UH, YEAH, I'M SERIOUS. WHAT HAPPENED TO THE WALL?"

Now I'm just as annoyed as her. Her looks and tone make my head throb harder. They make the RAGE want to bust through my skull. They make me want to hurl the fucking water jug at her. They make me want to fucking puke.

"I'LL TELL YOU WHAT HAPPENED. LAST NIGHT YOU CAME HOME SHIT-FACED AND STARTED BANGING ON OUR BEDROOM DOOR CALLING US NAMES AND THREATENING TO KILL US. YOU SAID YOU HAD A BUTCHER KNIFE AND YOU WERE GOING TO KILL US WITH IT. THEN WE HEARD CRASHING AND BANGING OUT HERE."

I stare at her. She must be fucking joking. My head throbs and throbs and searches for some sort of memory of the night.

Search. Think. Remember. Try. Try. Try. TRY.

Nothing. I can't remember anything.

I can feel my brain pulsating. I can feel my brain pulsating so hard and so fast that my skull feels like it's going to crack. I can't feel anything but the cracking and pulsating and pounding and confusion.

I can't remember anything. I can't remember anything but I know I'm not a violent person. I've never hit anyone in my life. Ever. I don't fucking believe her. She's full of fucking shit. I don't fucking trust her as far as I can fucking throw her. Seriously.

"YEAH, RIGHT MOM! WHAT-FUCKING-EVER!"

"YOU DID, ARABELLA. I DON'T EVEN WANT TO LOOK AT YOUR FACE RIGHT NOW. WHAT IS YOUR FUCKING PROBLEM, ARABELLA?!?!?! YOU NEED TO GET OUT OF MY SIGHT. RIGHT NOW!"

I look at Daryl.

"It's true, Arabella. You came home and threatened to kill us."

I start to shrink and pound and disappear into the couch. Disappear into my shame. My shame and disgust and pounding and hurt and humiliation and disgrace and . . .

"FUCK YOU GUYS!"

I run into my room and cry on my bed. I cry and try to remember. I try to think and remember and remember—please remember!

Nothing. Nothing. Nothing.

Nothing but horror and shame and disgust and pain.

I sob and sob and wish I was dead. I wish I was dead and so does everyone around me. I wish I was dead. I'm fucking disgusting and stupid and drunk and I blackout and I'm fucked up. I'm so fucked up. I can't live like this. I have to die. I have to find a way not to feel like this anymore.

I sob and sob and grab the fat on my thighs and the fat on my stomach and twist and cry out and think of how disgustingly fat and grotesque I am.

TEN TO ELEVEN YEARS OLD

I love this show. I love this show. This is my favorite show ever.

I love *The Cosby Show*. I wish my family was like them. I wish Bill Cosby was my dad and I wish my mom was like Claire Huxtable. I wish my brother was Theo and I wish that my sisters were like Sandra and Denise and Vanessa and Rudy.

I wish I could just jump into the TV and live there. I wish I could live there with them or live with the girls on *The Facts of Life*. I wish I had a mom like Barbara and Valerie's mom on *One Day at a Time*. A mom who cares and loves me like their mom does.

I wish that I could be adopted like Willis on *Different Strokes*. Adopted by some rich man who loved me and was nice to me. Not adopted like Bill adopted me.

I wish and wish and wish.

I lie on the couch and close my eyes and tap my feet together like Dorothy from *The Wizard of Oz*. And I wish. And wish. And wish. I picture being with the Tin Man and the Lion and the Scarecrow.

I open my eyes. I'm still here. I'm still here on my couch just watching the Cosbys. Oh well. At least I can watch them. They make me laugh.

I laugh because Bill Cosby is funny with his kids. I smile and grab my blanket and tuck it around my feet and watch and laugh.

"ARABELLA, GET UP HERE AND FEED THE DOGS!"

Awwwww man. I don't want to go feed the dogs yet. Geez. I just want to watch this show.

I call up to him.

"I'll come up at commercial break, okay?"

All of a sudden I hear stomping over my head. Loud stomping above my head and it's coming across the floor.

Oh no! He's coming to get me! He's coming to get me and he's gonna hit me and hurt me and smack me and punch me.

Why did I say that? Why didn't I just get up and go feed the dogs? I'm scared. I'm scared. I'm scared.

My heart is pounding and I want to hide under the covers. I want to jump into Bill Cosby's house and hide in Rudy's room. I'm gonna get hit. He's gonna come hit me; I can tell by the stomping of his feet. He's on a mission and his mission is to come punish me for talking back and not just doing what he says.

I'm scared. I'm scared. I'm scared and I can't move.

I see his feet and legs come down the stairs and I try to get myself up but I'm stuck. I can't move. I'm scared. I'm scared. Terror is in my stomach again. Terror and fear and scared and hide and run and hide and hide and hide.

My heart is in my throat now. I feel like my heart is trying to jump out of my throat. Out of my throat and I can't breathe. I can't breathe and my heart is stuck in my throat.

He gets to the bottom of the stairs and he looks like a mad man. He's crazed. He has that look that he gets whenever he wants to hit someone or hurt someone. I know that look. I've seen it before.

I shrink smaller and smaller into the couch. I want to disappear. I wish I could disappear. I wish and wish and pray and I'm scared. I'm scared and just want to hide. Hide. Hide. Hide.

All I feel is terror. He's stomping towards me with that look like he's going to pound my face in. He's going to hurt me so I have to brace myself.

I tighten all of my muscles and get ready for the beating to begin. I get ready for the punishment. I wish I wouldn't have talked back. I wish I wouldn't have talked back. I wish I wouldn't have talked back.

My heart is still in my throat and now I have a sick feeling in my stomach. I'm terrified. I can't move. I just tighten and tighten and wish and wish and wish I wouldn't have been a brat. I brace myself and sink further into the couch.

I shouldn't have said anything. I shouldn't have said anything cuz then this wouldn't be happening. I should've just done what I was supposed to do. I wish I would've done what I was supposed to do and then he wouldn't come hit me.

He towers above me like a building. He towers above me and I see his arm move up.

I can't breathe. I can't breathe and I freeze and tighten and wait for the hitting. The pounding. The punching and the hitting and the pounding. He towers above me like a building and I shrink more. I'm shrinking and shrinking and can't breathe and can't breathe and bracing myself for the hitting to begin.

He grabs me by the front of my shirt and rips me off of the couch. He doesn't say anything. He doesn't say a thing. He rips me off of the couch by my shirt and my legs slam against the coffee table. My legs slam against the coffee table and I cry out and he doesn't care. It makes him madder and he takes his other hand and grabs the other side of my shirt.

His face is twisted in RAGE. Twisted and RAGE and he wants to kill me and hurt me and punish me.

"YOU'LL FEED THE DOGS WHEN I SAY YOU WILL FEED THE GODDAMN DOGS!"

I start to cry harder. I can't breathe and I'm crying and my throat is tight and my neck is burning from the shirt strangling me. I feel like I'm dying as the shirt is tightening around my neck.

He stomps across the floor and drags me by my shirt. I can't breathe because the shirt is strangling me and tightening and I'm crying and the crying is making my throat lumpy and I feel like I'm going to die. I can hear my tears sizzling and frying as they slide down my throbbing, fiery cheeks.

He drags me up the stairs by the shirt. And as he drags me, I can't breathe more and more. Less and less. There is less and less air that I can find. The shirt is so tight around my neck that it feels like a rope. It feels like the rope that Dave has around his teddy bear's neck that's hanging in his bedroom. It's tightening more and more and it won't stop and I start to see stars.

"YOU'LL FEED THE DOGS WHEN I TELL YOU TO FEED THE FUCKING DOGS!"

My body thumps up each step as he pulls me up them by my shirt. My legs drag and I try to get a grip on the floor and try to stand so that I can breathe. So that the shirt will stop tightening around my neck. Stop squeezing and squeezing and suffocating me.

So that I will survive and not pass out and then get hit for passing out.

I can't get a grip on the stairs. He's dragging me too fast up them. Too fast and too hard and too tight.

I can't breathe and I can't breathe and I can't breathe. I see spots. White little spots like little mosquitoes flying all around me.

RIP!

I look down and the buttons on my shirt are starting to pop off. Rip off. He's dragging me and ripping me and I can see my bra.

I can't let him see my bra! He can't see my bra! He can't see my bra!

RIP!

Another button.

RIP! RIP!

Two more buttons and now there is only one left. My bra and my stomach and my chest are all showing and I don't care that I can't breathe or that my neck feels like there is a blister the size of a huge rope around it or that my face is being burnt by my tears or that I'm seeing the little white mosquitoes. He can't see my chest! He can't see my bra!

He gets me to the top of the stairs and my shirt is completely ripped open except for the one button on the bottom. It's completely ripped open and my neck is burning like someone has a lighter on it. Like someone has stuck cigarettes up to it and is burning all of the skin off of it. But all I care about is the bra and him not seeing it.

He throws me by my shirt at the top of the stairs and I slam against the ground.

RIP!

The last button is gone. I am totally showing and crying and burning and humiliated and terrified and I wish I was dead.

He towers above me and looks at me with disgust.

"GET IN THERE AND FEED THE FUCKING DOGS! AND STOP YOUR FUCKING CRYING OR I'LL GIVE YOU SOMETHING TO CRY ABOUT! YOU'RE SUCH A CRY BABY! WAAA-WAAAA-WAAA! ALL YOU EVER DO IS CRY!"

I pull myself up off the ground and turn towards the kitchen and wait for him to hit me from behind. I tighten and wait and the tears are unstoppable. The tears are a constant hot flood searing my cheeks.

I grab my shirt and look down. I look down through the blur of the hot, watery humiliation and the fear in my eyes. I look down and grab the sides of my shirt and try to pull them together and they won't stay because he ripped all of the buttons off of them.

I force myself to make no noise as I cry and walk to the garage to get the dog food. My body sobs and jerks with deep, fearful, humiliated sobs. No matter how hard I try to hold back the sobbing, my body is bumping up and down and I can't breathe.

I scoop the dog food and try to hold back the tears. I'm a big fat cry baby. A big fat cry baby. I bump up and down and up and down and try to breathe and sob and try to breathe and try not to cry.

I try to hold back the tears and hold the front of my shirt together.

He saw my bra. He saw my chest. He saw my bra and my skin and he knows what I look like down there now. He knows what I look like and I want to hide. I want to hide because I'm disgusting and bad. Bad and a baby.

All I feel is humiliation and shame and burning and anger and disgust and fear and humiliation. Humiliation. Humiliation. Humiliation.

I wish someone would save me. I wish my mom would leave him. I wish that someone would save me.

I wish that I could jump into the TV and have the other Bill as my dad.

TWENTY-NINE YEARS OLD

(Day One, 5:35 p.m.)

I pace back and forth and back and forth. My friends have left and now I just wait. I wait and pace and the panic wells and grows and bubbles and takes over my body.

I feel lightheaded. I feel tingly. I feel like I'm going to hyperventilate. I suck in shallow breaths and with each one I pace faster and faster across the hardwood floors. I can't breathe. I can't fucking breathe. I CAN'T FUCKING BREATHE!

I try to make sense of all of this. How could this be? I think back to all of the conversations that we've had about this and I think that he must have only been doing *it* recently. There's no way he could have been doing *it* the whole time. No fucking way.

That would be too many lies. Too much for him to cover up. He doesn't have it in him to be *that* deceptive.

I pace and breathe faster and panic and pace and I feel like I'm going to explode. Nothing seems real. Everything is floating around me like a dizzy dream. This can't be happening. This can't be happening. This can't be fucking happening!

Then I think about the computer. I think about the password and I feel Rage. Fucking RAGE. Something is going on. What the fuck is going on?!?!? None of this makes sense. None of it at all. Why would he have a password? What else is he hiding?

And the lying starts again in a swirl of confusion. Maybe he just doesn't want Jon logging on in his name. Maybe he . . .

I can't come up with any other maybes. I can't think of any other logical explanation as to why he would have a password.

And so the RAGE hits again.

Maybe he's a fucking liar. Maybe everything has been a lie. Maybe. That's a fucked-up maybe.

And so I lie to myself again.

But, he isn't like that. No way. He can't be that guy. NO WAY!!!

He isn't like those other guys. There's something about him that's special. Fucking special. I have done too much work on myself to end up with someone who could deceive me this way. I couldn't have attracted someone into my life who would do this. Not this. No way. No fucking how. Or could I?

I grab my hair and crouch down onto my knees and scream at the top of my lungs.

"AAAAAAAGGGGGHHHHHHHHHHHHHHHHHH!"

I'm frantic and panicky and my head is swirling. Everything is blurry and wrong and swirling. Fucking swirling. Everything feels unreal. Like in a scary dream. Like the scary dreams that I've had all my life.

Like the scary dream that I had two nights ago.

FLASH!
SMACK!

I wake up like I usually do after a nightmare. Crying and feeling like the horror that I just dreamed was real. I lie in bed and cry and think about the horrible dream and try to tell myself that it was just a dream. Steve would never do that to me. He loves me. I tell myself that I've had those kinds of dreams all through growing up—all the time—and it's just my fears. It's just me being scared.

Then I think about the dream. I see him. And I see her. She's gorgeous. She's this little, petite, Asian-Indian looking girl. She's a lot younger than I am. She's a few years younger than Steve. She's stunning and he loves her and tells me he wants to be with her and that he's been with her when I wasn't around.

I cry. I cry and think about how many times I've dreamt of him with other women. I cry and then I get angry with myself for having these dreams. I tell myself how insecure and stupid I'm being. I cry and tell myself that he loves me. I cry and think of how many times he's woken me up while I was yelling in my sleep and he would hold me and tell me none of it was true. That he would never hurt me. He loves me and he would never do that to me. He would never.

Ever . . .

Normally I can shake off the dreams. Normally. But that one I couldn't. For some reason. For some reason that one stuck with me and made my stomach feel sick and made me wonder. Something was going on. I didn't know what. But something made me tear apart his room.

I stay crouched on my knees and cry and think that nothing is making sense. I bounce. I bounce off the walls. Each wall is a different emotion. And each wall thrusts me into another wall. Another wall that's waiting for me. Another wall that's waiting to smack me hard with another emotion and then hurl me with vengeance to the next wall, the next emotion.

I am gone. I am fucking gone. I am gone and nothing is real. I know nothing. I know nothing anymore. Anyfuckingmore.

I no longer exist. Who I thought I was is no longer me.

She's gone.
She's lost.
I can't find her.

FOURTEEN YEARS OLD

We sing.

Our Father

Who art in Heaven

Hallowed be Thy name.

Our Kingdom come

Thy will be done

On Earth as it is

In Heaven.

Give us this day—

I start to see stars. I start to feel dizzy and hot and I see stars. I start to get a tingly feeling in my face and my fingers and there are little white dots flying around my face.

The huge Jesus hanging on the cross in front of me is getting black. Everything's getting blacker. Oh fuck, everything's getting black.

Everything goes bla—

I open my eyes and see faces all above me and around me. There's light shining from behind them. Light shining from behind their heads and faces looking at me with love and concern and question. Maybe they're angels. I don't know where I am. There's light and faces and they're all around me.

I hear one of them speak.

"Are you okay, Arabella?"

It's my mom.

I'm feeling tingly and dizzy still and I'm unsure what's going on.

"Where am I?"

"We're at church. You passed out during the singing of the Lord's Prayer."

"Oh."

I rub my eyes and try to sit up. I feel arms around me helping me sit up in the pew. I feel dizzy and sick to my stomach. I feel hot. I feel hot and hotter, like I need to be dunked in ice water.

I pull up my dangling head and look to my side. There are faces all over and my mom and the Priest and curiosity and light. They're wondering—like I'm wondering—what's going on.

"Mom, I'm really hot. I'm burning up."

"Okay, let's go outside."

My mom grabs one arm and someone else grabs the other. They help me up and as we walk up the aisle and toward the doors I hear whispering and feel stares. Everyone is staring at me and whispering and wondering.

We get outside and my mom and the other person sit me on the ground next to the huge pine tree outside of the church.

I feel a slight breeze on my face and it feels good. It's a warm breeze, but it feels better than no breeze at all and definitely better than being stared at by all those people.

"Are you going to be okay?"

I look over and the other person is sitting next to me. It's the Priest.

I'm embarrassed and uncomfortable and I want him to go back inside and leave me alone with the breeze and my sick stomach and my mom.

"I'll be okay. Thanks for helping me out here. I'm sorry that I messed up church."

"Oh, you didn't mess anything up. You sit here with your mother and enjoy the sunshine and get some fresh air, okay?"

"Okay. Sorry again."

"There's no need for you to be sorry, my dear."

He gets up and starts walking towards the church.

"God bless you, my child."

"God bless you, too."

I always feel so fucking weird saying that to people. Especially a Priest. If he knew what I was really like then he wouldn't be blessing me at all.

I take a deep breath and feel my skin cooling down a little bit. I feel the breeze and the evening sun on my face. It feels so much better to be out here.

"What happened, Arabella? Why did you pass out?"

"I don't know, Mom. I didn't have breakfast this morning, that's probably what it is."

"Yeah, you know I'm hypoglycemic and if I don't eat every few hours I get sick too. I just didn't know you got like that."

"I guess I do, Mom."

I don't tell her that I'm going on my third day without food. I don't tell her that I can't eat because I'm fucking fat and disgusting and I have to lose weight so that I can feel better. I don't tell her that when I look in the mirror I want to slice the fat off of my thighs. I don't tell her that I feel like passing out all of the time.

I don't tell her any of this because she doesn't understand.

She doesn't understand because she's little and skinny and petite. She can eat.

I'm BIG and fat and disgusting and I have to starve myself. I can't eat. I can't eat. I can't eat.

I don't tell her any of this because she doesn't understand.

She's not BIG.

TWELVE YEARS OLD

"HELP ME! STOP! HELP! HELP! HELP!"

I open my eyes and the bedroom is dark. I hear screaming. Blood-curdling screaming.

It's my mom. Again.

Then, "YOU FUCKING BITCH! YOU FUCKING WHORE! I'M GOING TO FUCKING KILL YOU!"

"STOP, BILL! STOP PLEEEEAAAASE!"

I lie in my bed and feel my heart start to go. Faster and faster and faster. I lie there and fear for what I should do.

Should I get up and go see what's happening? I can't move, though. I can't move because my body is frozen. It's glued to the bed. Glued to the bed and I can't move.

There's more screaming and I hear flesh hitting flesh. The sound of punching and kicking and beating. The same sound that I've heard before from another room.

"HELP! STOP! PLEASE STOP!"

"FUCK YOU, YOU STUPID FUCKING BITCH!"

I lie in the dark. My heart races and I want to get up and help but at the same time, I don't. I hate him for hitting us. I hate him for being in our house. I hate him with every fiber in my body. I hate him more and more with every scream.

I hate her too. I hate her for staying with him. I hate her for being such a wimp. I hate her for letting him hit us. I hate her for being so weak that she won't leave him. I fucking hate her. I hate her for all the times this has happened and all the times I try to help.

FLASH!

He has her by the shirt and he's dragging her out the front door and kicking her and telling her what a fucking bitch she is.

It's the middle of the night and the neighbors are all asleep and the screaming is going to wake them up.

She's calling my name and begging me to help her. He's throwing her out the door. She's holding onto the doorframe and trying to stay in the house.

I jump on his back and try to get him off of her. I'm RAGEful and I want to kill him. I want to fucking kill him for being such a fucking asshole and trying to throw her out the door.

He moves his arm and grabs me off of his back and throws me onto the loveseat. I can't breathe. I can't breathe because when I hit the seat all of the air knocked out of my body.

The next day my neighbor friends tell me that their whole family was awakened by my parents yelling at our dogs. Yeah, right. The fucking dogs. I could tell by the look on their faces that they knew that was bullshit. I fucking hate this family . . .

I lie in the bed and hear the pathetic screams. His crazy RAGE. RAGE and PATHETIC SCREAMS. That's all I hear. There aren't even words anymore, just raw emotion vibrating through the house, down the hall, and into my room.

I feel Rage. RAGE and fear. And it keeps me glued to the bed.

With every one of her screams I get more and more angry and more and more glued to the bed. More and more fearful and angry and my heart beats faster and faster and I need to get the hell out of here. I need to go find somewhere else to be. I need to hide and get away. I need to find another family to live with.

I hear the door slam and then nothing.

Quiet.

Then begins the pathetic calls for help. Whimpering, desperate cries.

"Arabella, help me!"

Cry. Cry. Sob. Sob. Sob.

"Help me, Arabella. Please. I can't move. My neck hurts. I can't move."

Cry and sob and pathetic little cry.

I lay in bed and the RAGE wells inside of me. You deserve this, you fucking bitch. If you would've left him years ago, this wouldn't be happening. I don't care if you're out there crying and hurt. You put yourself into this situation, and you can get your pathetic little self out. I'm tired of being the one who gives you advice just so you can shit on it and do what you're going to do anyway.

FLASH!

We're out in the garage. She's got her bright pink cup with her vodka and she's smoking her minty cigarettes.

Like the million other times, she tells me that I'm her best friend and she loves me so much and that I'm her best friend. And then I start to counsel her.

She asks me what she should do.

I tell her to leave him. We'll be fine. Somehow we'll be okay. We can get help from the church and friends and other places. We don't need him.

"I don't know what to do, Arabella. Tell me it's going to be okay."

She says that all the time. Tell me what I should do and tell me it's going to be okay. And since the fourth grade that's what I've been doing. Telling her what to do and that everything will be okay . . .

As I lie glued to the bed I feel the RAGE welling inside of me. RAGE and hatred and frustration and wrath and I want to tear the house apart. I hear her pathetic cries for help and I want her to suffer. I want her to suffer like she's made me suffer. I want her to lie there and feel the suffering and the aloneness and the betrayal of knowing that someone is in the other room who could save her but that person is doing nothing. Ignoring her. Acting as if she doesn't hear what's going on.

I want her to lie there waiting for someone to come save her like I've waited for someone to come save me.

Like I've waited for her to come save me.

TWENTY-FIVE YEARS OLD

I drive the truck off of the ferry and she tells me how scared she is. How scared she is to tell Eva about what's been going on.

I tell her that I'm scared too but that it has to be done. We have to come clean. And everything will be okay.

I always tell her that everything will be okay. For as long as I can remember I've told her that everything will be okay.

This is the second time that she's come to Savannah to visit me. The second time, and I've lived here for six years. I've gone back to visit her at least once a year since I moved here.

She's agreed to come out to Savannah to do some therapy with me. Three hours a day for five days. Somehow Eva managed to convince her to come out here. It's a fucking miracle.

We drive and worry. Drive and worry. I'm worried because I love Eva and I don't want her to be disappointed in me. My mom worries because she has to come clean and face the fact that she has a major problem.

We pull up to the therapy office and we walk inside.

We sit down in her office and feel the throbbing in our heads and the thirst of our bodies.

Eva asks us how we're doing.

I look at my mom and see that I'm going to have to take the lead. As usual.

I take a deep breath and start to tell the story.

"Well, Eva. First of all, I've been drinking. For the last few months I've been drinking and not telling you about it. I haven't done any drugs, but I have been drinking. And after last night, I know that I can't do it anymore."

I take a deep breath and search her eyes for the disappointment.

There is none. Just love and compassion. So I continue.

"Well, last night my mom and I decided to get some wine. We finished a bottle and decided to go out and get some more."

I look at my mom. She has that look of the scolded little child who's about to get in trouble. I take a deep breath and continue.

"Well, we were on our second bottle when Keith called and said that he wanted to come over. He had his son with him. By the time he got there, my mom was really shit-faced."

Eva looks over at my mom. My mom looks ashamed. She looks like a scolded child who got caught doing something she wasn't supposed to. Her pathetic-little-child look.

I continue.

"We sat down to eat dinner and she was swaying in her seat and slurring her words and she had that bug-eyed look she gets when she's wasted.

"She was trying to talk to Keith's ten-year-old son, Andrew, about something and she couldn't even put a sentence together.

"Andrew was really uneasy. He looked nervous and totally uncomfortable. I was embarrassed and totally humiliated and worried about Andrew.

"Then she tried to get up and walk to the kitchen to get another piece of chicken."

I look at my mom and take a deep breath and get ready to tell Eva.

I continue.

"She staggered to the stove and as she grabbed a piece of chicken, she fell into the trash can and folded in half like a clothes pin."

I look at my mom and she looks humiliated. Shame and humiliation and regret and embarrassment. She feels it all and I can see it in her face.

I continue.

"Well, she was stuck. She was stuck and laughing and screaming and Andrew was horrified. The look in his eyes was enough to make me want to fucking die.

"My mom got shit-faced in front of my new boyfriend and his son and I wanted to fucking die!"

I take a deep breath and get ready to tell her about yesterday morning. I didn't tell my mom that I was going to tell Eva this. But I have to. I have to because this is my mom. This is who she is and she won't change if it's not brought to her attention.

I continue.

"So yesterday morning, my mom, Keith, and I were having breakfast and somehow the subject of hair color came up."

I look at my mom and I can tell that she doesn't want me to tell Eva, but I have to. I don't care what she wants; this needs to be said. This is who she is and what I grew up with and it's relevant to my therapy.

"Mom, I know you don't want me to bring this up, but I have to."

I look at Eva and continue.

"So, the subject of hair color came up and I said that this was my natural hair color. And then I said that I wish my mom would wear her hair in its natural color, which is dark brown like mine."

I take another deep breath and feel the humiliation welling in me. I feel ashamed of her and embarrassed and I think that Eva's going to think that I'm like her. That I would say stuff like that because my mom says stuff like that. I feel shame and embarrassment and humiliation and worry that Eva won't see me the same way. She'll see me as my mom.

I continue.

"So, Keith says, 'Oh, that's not your real hair color?' And her response was 'No, honey. If you want to see my natural hair color you'll have to look somewhere else.' And she started laughing her hysterical, annoying laugh."

I look at her and look at Eva.

Eva's eyes are wide with surprise. My mom is hanging her head in shame.

I continue.

"I was mortified. He was mortified. She was the only one who didn't see that she was being completely and totally inappropriate, to put it mildly."

I take another deep breath and the floodgates open.

"She basically just told my boyfriend that he needs to look at her pubic hair to find her real hair color! She does this shit all of the time. She's always flirted with my boyfriends and tried to get them to see her as sexy. Like with Sean. She was hanging all over him once when she was shit-faced. She had her arm around him and her face right next to his. And he told me later that night that she was trying to get him to tell her how pretty she was the whole time she was hanging on him. And me and Daryl were walking right in front of her!"

I stop and look over and see that my mom is crying. She has that pathetic, little-child, manipulation face on.

Eva looks at her.

"Are you okay, Rachel?"

"No," she sobs. "No, I'm not okay. I feel horrible that I made Arabella feel like this. I know that I need to stop drinking. I know that I act stupid when I do. I know—"

"MOM, you weren't even drunk when you made the pubic hair comment! You do this shit all the time. ALL THE TIME. It's not just the alcohol. You disappear from my life for months on end. You disappear if I'm not right in front of you. You forget about me. You don't call. When you do call, all you do is talk about yourself. You say stupid shit. You sent me to get molested every summer. You married abusive assholes and let them beat us. You were the child and I was the mother. You never did anything to build my self-esteem. You told me I was BIG all the time. You compared yourself to me. You called me a slut and didn't talk to me for months when I was spiraling out of control in my drug addiction. It's fucking everything. Fucking everything! Not just the booze. It's fucking everything. You disappear. You're not a mom and you never have been!"

I stop and look at her.

She's sobbing now. Sobbing and it's all my fault. I've made her feel like shit. This is why she disappears. I tell her how she hurt me and she disappears. I feel like shit. I shouldn't tell her what she's done, because then she ends up crying and I end up feeling like I'm a bad daughter.

"You're attacking and abusing me, Arabella."

Sob. Sob. Fucking sob.

Eva looks at her. She looks at me. She looks back at her.

"It's okay if you need to stop, Rachel, and get your feelings taken care of."

"Okay."

Sob, sob, pathetic fucking sob.

"But I want to tell you something. It may have felt like Arabella was being abusive, but she was just telling you how she felt. She didn't call you names or try to hurt you. She was just telling you things that you did that have impacted and hurt her. She was telling you her experience of growing up with you."

My mom looks up. She's sobbing more and more.

She's doing her manipulative, feel-sorry-for-me sobs to divert attention away from taking responsibility for what she's done. And I feel sorry for her the whole time I'm thinking this. I feel sorry for her and I feel like I'm a bitch of a daughter every time I tell her that she's hurt me. Because she cries and I end up having to make her feel better. And then I feel like smacking her because I'm tired of taking care of her feelings. That's all I've ever done and it's *my* fucking turn to have *her* take care of *me*.

There's more talking and more crying and more manipulation and more of me feeling like a horrible bitch of a daughter. There's more RAGE and anger and exhaustion and feeling like I always take care of her.

It's always the same. I'm either a bitch who hurts her or RAGE-ful because of her. I'm a bitch when she cries.

On the drive home she asks me for a cigarette. She usually doesn't smoke unless she's been drinking. I know I've hurt her. I know I'm a fucking bitch for telling her what she's done wrong.

At a stoplight, she looks at me and grabs my hand and tells me to look at her. She kisses my hand and tells me that she's never going to disappear again. She has tears in her eyes and I think she means it.

She says, "Arabella, I promise you I will never put a man above you again. I promise you that I will not disappear. I promise you that I will be your mother from now on. I promise you that when I'm not around you, you will not disappear. Do you believe me?"

I look into her brown teary eyes and see the sincerity in them. I see the sincerity and feel love for her. I feel hope and I feel cared about.

I feel hope.

"Yes, I believe you."

And she lived up to her word.

She lived up to her word for about ten days.

She called me and told me how special I was and asked how I was doing and really cared about me for the first time in my life.

And then my brother got out of jail. And I needed to talk to her. And she told me that she had company and that I was a baby and that was the last time I would hear her voice.

Ever.

TWENTY-THREE YEARS OLD

What was that? What was that? What was that?

What was that fucking noise? I hear voices. I hear something. There's something out there. There's someone out there. Someone's coming up on the deck. Someone's coming up on the deck. Shit. Fuck. Shit. Fuck. Fuck, fuck, fuck.

Who would be coming on the deck right now? Who? Why? Huh? Huh? Who would be coming on my deck? Fuck, fuck, fuck, fuck.

I jump up from the bed and get up close to the window like a crazed, paranoid, wild woman. I hold my breath and don't breathe so I can hear the voices.

I hear them. I hear them and I know they're out there and they're coming to get me.

I take my finger and lightly touch the blinds. I want to pull them apart to look, but if I do, then they'll see me. They'll see me and then they'll know I'm in here. They can't see me. I can't have them see me. No way. No how. Nuh-uh. No. No. Can't. No.

There are little tiny holes in the blinds where the string holds them together. There are little tiny holes and I can look through those. Little tiny holes. I'll look through those and then they won't see me seeing them.

I peek through the tiny holes. There's no one there. No one I can see, but I hear footsteps and voices. I hear them and they're coming from somewhere. I don't know where, but I know they're there and they're coming to get me. I know it.

Uh-huh. Uh-huh. They are coming. Coming to get me. Coming. To get me.

No. I'm just hallucinating because I'm detoxing. It's just the meth and the booze moving its way out of my—

Fuck! What was that?!?!?!?! There's someone out there, I know it. Uh-huh. I know it. They're coming to get me.

Uh-huh, uh-huh, uh-huh.

TWENTY-THREE YEARS OLD

I look down on the counter.

I look at my hands. I look at my hands and they shake. They shake and shake and I know it's time for more.

My neck cramps. My neck is cramping. Cramping. Cramping. Cramping. Like usual.

I look down on the counter and pull my compact out of the drawer. My Max Factor compact. I flip it open. I need more. I have to have more. It's been over an hour and I need more. More. More. More.

I pull out the razor. I pull out the razor and one of the yellow rocks. I pull out the yellow rock and set it on the counter.

I take a deep breath through my nose and think about it going up and want it and need it and think about how good it'll feel when it hits the back of my throat. I think about it and want it and need it. I need some more now. Have to have more now. Now. Now. Now.

I take the razor and I smash the rock. I smash the rock on the counter and get ready to chop and chop and chop and line it up.

I look over at the clock. It's 8 a.m. and I'm already on my third line since I woke up an hour and a half ago. I only slept for two hours last night. So it's okay if I do this much. It's not that much more than usual. I'm only at eight or nine lines a day. That's not that fucking bad.

At least I'm not shooting it. At least I'm still working. Fuck, I'm at work right now and I'm fine. I'm fine. I'm fucking fine. I go to work. I workout. I pay my bills. I do what needs to be done and at least I do that. It'd be a fucking problem if I couldn't make it to work. That's when I'll know that I have a problem.

I chop and chop and move the powder around into little lines. I look at the powder.

I need more. I need more to maintain. It's not about getting high. I just need it to maintain. Need it. Have to have it.

At least I'm skinny. I don't care. I'm skinny and I can eat whatever I want and I work and guys want me. I can get a different guy every night. I'm skinny and pretty and guys like me and that's all that matters.

I push the powder into lines. But they aren't big enough so I move them into one another. I push them into one another so that there are half as many. Two big, fucking lines. Two, big, thick, yellow lines. Two fucking big lines of cleaning fluid and chemicals and nasty shit that keeps me skinny. That's enough for now. Now. For now.

I pull out the straw and notice that it's got a crack in it. I notice that there's a crack in the fucking straw. Fuck. Fuck. Fuck.

But Mark has straws in his cabinet. I rush over to the cabinet. I have to get it. I have to get the straw and cut it and snort. Cut it and snort. I have to snort. I have to get the straw.

I get the straw and the scissors and cut it into a three-inch-long piece. Long enough to fit in the compact. Long enough. Long enough to snort it up. Long enough to snort it. Snort. Snort and snort.

I look out the kitchen window and make sure that no one can see me. Make sure that no one sees me snort.

It's safe. No one's there. No one's there and I can snort.

I walk over to the counter and bend down and stick my nose to the straw and up my nostril. I take a finger and hold the other nostril closed.

And I inhale. Quick and hard and clean and deep. I suck the whole thick line up and feel it hit the back of my throat. It hits the back of my throat and it tastes like shit and I swallow.

I stand myself up and inhale and let the drip start. The drip starts and it tastes like shit. Nasty and chemicals and nasty. Nasty, burning, nasty. But I don't care. It's worth it.

I lean down again and go for the second line. I stick the straw up the other nostril. I stick the straw up and suck. Quick and clean and deep and hard.

I stand up. That's enough.

For now.

SEVEN TO NINE YEARS OLD
House on Squirrel Road

I sit on the hill and pet Joker. I pet Joker cuz I love him and he's a nice doggy. And he's my doggy. He's big and brown and nice and mine. Well, he's the whole family's, but that means he's mine. And he's nice to me.

Dave sits down next to me. He's smiling.

"What are you doing, Arabella?"

He says it really nice. He's never really nice to me. But he's being nice and not mean so I smile at him and say, "Nothing. I'm just pettin' Joker."

I look at Joker and pet him and rub him behind his ears. He likes it and his tongue goes out of his mouth and he smiles too. We are all smiling. We are all sitting on the hill in the sun and smiling. I like it.

Dave walks over to a bunch of tall, brown grassy stuff and picks a couple of them. He comes back and sits down next to me.

"Hey, Arabella, I got a game to play, okay?"

I look at him. He's smiling in a funny way.

I feel kinda funny. I wonder if he's really being nice to me.

"What game, Dave?"

He takes the long, brown grassy stuff and crosses one of them over the other. He puts one over the other so that they look like an X.

He smiles again and tells me to bite down on it where it crosses.

I get that funny feeling in my tummy that I get when I'm scared. It's icky and turning and I do not like it. I get it when people do something mean to me.

I do not want to bite down on it.

"Come on, Arabella. Just do it. It'll be fun."

I do not want to. It's not gonna be fun.

"Come on. It's not going to hurt you, I swear."

I look at him and look at his eyes and his face. I look at his eyes and his face to see if he's got meanness in him that he's trying to not let me see. His face is straight. He don't look like he is trying to be mean but my tummy still feels icky.

"I don't want to, Dave."

"C'mon, Arabella. This is a fun game. It's really fun. It's not going to hurt you. It's just wheat; how could it hurt you? I'm not going to do something to hurt you, I swear."

I look in his eyes again and at his mouth and see if he has the meanness in him.

"You swear?"

I want him to tell me he's going to be nice to me and will not hurt me again before I play the game.

"I swear. It's just a game. I just played it with Eddie and he had fun. I swear it's not going to hurt you."

"You swear on Mom's life and cross your heart and hope to die and stick a needle in your eye?"

"Yes, I swear. I swear. I wouldn't hurt you. You're my little sister. I just want to play a game with you."

"Say you cross your heart and hope to die and stick a needle in your eye, Dave."

He looks at me, annoyed.

"Arabella, I cross my heart and hope to die and stick a needle in my eye if I'm lying. Okay? Can we play the game now?"

My tummy still feels icky, but he says that he will stick a needle in his eye. So I believe him.

"You ready?"

"Yeah, I'm ready."

He takes the grass and holds it like an X.

"Okay, Arabella. When I stick this in your mouth, bite down on it when I tell you, okay?"

"Okay. You are not gonna hurt me, right?"

"No, Arabella. I'm not gonna hurt you. I already told you. Okay?"

My tummy still feels icky. But he said he will not hurt me, so I'll do it anyway.

I open my mouth and he sticks the X in my mouth. He tells me to bite down.

I bite down on it.

"Are you ready?"

I shake my head up and down. But my tummy still feels icky.

He yanks on the ends of the grass.

I can't breathe. I can't breathe. There are tons of prickly and sticky things in my throat and I can't breathe. I can't breathe. I try to take a breath and all of a sudden all of the prickly, sticky pieces go further down my throat and I'm choking.

I'm scared. I can't breathe and I can't swallow and I'm gonna die. I need to breathe and I can't, cuz when I try to suck in air, all of the prickles and stickies go further down my throat.

The prickles and stickies are cutting and stabbing my throat and my tubes that go to my stomach. They are sticking and cutting and stabbing and I can't breathe.

I start to cry and get scared that I'm gonna die cuz I can't breathe in and I need to breathe in so that I don't die. Breathe and die and cry and can't breathe and desperate and dizzy. I'm getting dizzy cuz I know I'm gonna die and I can't breathe.

I hear Dave laughing. But I can't see him, cuz all I can see are tears and water and scariness. I'm scared. I'm scared. I'm scared. I'm scared. I'm gonna die. I'm gonna die. I'm gonna die.

All I see is water and scaredness and I can't breathe and there are stickies in my throat and they are stabbing and cutting and choking and strangling and suffocating and I'm gonna die.

And he even stuck a needle in his eye.

TEN YEARS OLD

I hop into the hot tub right behind her.

I hop in and it feels warm and bubbly and good.

I'm at Jen's house. I'm at Jen's huge house in the woods. There's snow all over the ground and the trees and all over the lid to the hot tub. It's cold out and I can see my breath. Her parents are upstairs somewhere.

"You wanna play truth or dare, Arabella?"

"Sure."

We've played this game before and we both know what it means.

"I'll ask first."

"Okay."

I say okay cuz I don't care who goes first. I know where the game ends up, so I don't care.

"Truth, dare, double dare, promise, or repeat?"

"Umm, how about dare?"

"Okay. I dare you to French kiss me."

I look at her and giggle. She giggles too.

"Okay, come here."

We look around to make sure that no one's in the windows.

I put my mouth up to hers and kiss her lips. Then we both open our mouths and start to French kiss. We kiss for a long time. Our tongues move around in each other's mouths. My privates start to get warm and start to feel good. I like to play this game with her because we both end up feeling really good. We both end up having that explosion happen.

We finish our kiss and giggle.

"Okay, it's my turn. Truth, dare, double dare, promise, or repeat?"

"Double dare."

"Oooooh, double dare!"

I sit and think of what I want her to do to me. I feel how warm it's getting between my legs and I know what to tell her.

"Okay, I double dare you to kiss me down there."

She giggles. She's ready.

And so am I.

TWENTY-EIGHT YEARS OLD

I stare at the TV. I stare at the TV.

I cry. I cry. I cry.

I look at the clock. It's 5:30 p.m. I've been lying here since 11:00 a.m. I'm so fucked up. This is so fucked up. I'm never going to amount to anything. I am nothing. Nothing. NOTHING. NOTHING!!!

I stare at the TV and think about how to do it. How can I stop this pain? How to stop the constant pain and aloneness. I can't fucking feel this way anymore. I can't. I can't. I just can't fucking do this anymore.

I thought that my life would be better when I got sober. I thought that I would feel good. I thought that the pain might lessen a little bit. Just a little fucking bit. That's all.

I scream.

"GOD, WHY THE HELL CAN'T MY LIFE BE BETTER? WHY DO I FEEL LIKE FUCKING SHIT ALL THE TIME? I'VE BEEN SOBER FOR OVER FOUR YEARS AND I'M STILL FUCKING DEPRESSED ALL THE TIME. GIVE ME ONE REASON WHY I SHOULDN'T GO TO THE STORE RIGHT FUCKING NOW AND BUY A BOTTLE OF PILLS!!!"

I stare at the TV and cry. I cry and wish I was dead. Fucking dead. I wish I was dead because nothing's getting better. I don't fucking understand this. I don't understand this at all.

I scream.

"FUUUUUCCCCKKKKKK!"

I'm in school. I'm a 4.0 student. I have a boyfriend who loves me. I have a beautiful house to live in. I have my health. I have sweet animals who I love and I still want to die. I still want to fucking die.

I cry and cry and cry and think about all of the abuse. I think about growing up in fear all the time. All the time. No break. It was always scary. All the time. No relief. Ever. Never.

I think about how stupid I feel now. How, compared to everyone else, I'm fucking stupid. I can't handle as much as other people. Everyone else seems to deal with things just fine. I can't handle life. Nothing makes me happy. Ever. Nothing ever makes me happy.

There's something wrong with me. My feelings get hurt and I'm sad and moody and different. Worse. I'm a fucking loser compared to other people. I just want to die. I want to fucking die.

I cry. I wail. I wail and cry and cry and sob and picture being in the Spirit world with God and Goddesses and my angels and Spirit teachers and guides. I feel relief. I feel relief and calm and peace and I want to be there. I want to be there with them so bad.

I want to go get pills. I want to go get pills. I want to kill myself and be with my angels and teachers and guides. I have to go get the pills. Now. I have to end this misery called life.

What if I don't die? What if I end up a fucking vegetable or brain-dead or have nerve damage? What about my animals? Who would take care of them? Who would take care of my animals? I could give them to Steve. He could take care of them.

What if things get better? What if a year from now everything is better? What if I'm meant for something great? What if I'm meant for something fucking great? Sometimes I feel like I'm meant for something great. What if that's true? What if?

Why did I go through all of this shit? I didn't go through all of the abuse and torture and suspense of growing up just to kill myself now. There has to be some reason that I went through all of this shit. I am meant to be here.

But I can't fucking take this anymore. I don't know how much longer I can take this. Seriously.

I scream.

"I CAN'T FUCKING TAKE THIS, GOD!! SERIOUSLY, GOD! I DON'T KNOW HOW MUCH LONGER I CAN TAKE THIS. I'M TWO SECONDS AWAY FROM GOING

TO SEVEN ELEVEN AND BUYING A BOTTLE OF PILLS. I NEED A FUCKING SIGN. A FUCKING SIGN! IF YOU WANT ME ALIVE, I NEED YOU TO GIVE ME A SIGN RIGHT NOW! PLEASE!"

I cry and wait. I cry and wait for some sign from Spirit.

I cry some more and stare at the TV.

Nothing. Nothing.

Nothing.

Okay, God. Fine. Fuck this! It's over.

I run up the stairs and grab my keys out of the basket. I put my shoes on and start to walk towards the door.

Out of the corner of my eye I see my little Bug. He's on my bed. He looks at me with his pretty, crossed blue eyes and stretches. He stretches and yawns and looks deep into my eyes.

I walk over to him and scratch him on his head. He starts to purr. He starts to purr and tries to grab my hand with his paws. He grabs my hand with his paws and starts to kiss them. He licks them and kisses them like he does at night. At night when he comes and sleeps on the pillow next to me, he grabs my hands and kisses them.

I start to cry and know that he's my sign.

TWENTY-THREE YEARS OLD

I look to my right and my left. Where's a fucking bathroom? FUCK. Where's a fucking bathroom? Fuck. Fuck. Fuck.

I gotta find some place to do a line before I meet with my lawyer. The last one wasn't enough. It's been at least half an hour since the last one. I gotta do more. Now. More. More. More.

Before I go into that courtroom. I gotta have some more before I go face my fucking sentence. I'm too nervous to go without more. I need some fucking powder courage.

I turn right and find a little shit-hole bar to go into. I jump out of the car and walk inside and ask for the bathroom. The bartender points to the back of the bar.

I walk in and wait for the stall to open. I wait for the stall to open. I wait against the wall and bite my nails and wait and wait and hurry the fuck-up already!

She comes out and I rush in. I rush in and sit down as if I'm using the toilet and wait for her to wash her hands and get the fuck out. I wait for her to wash her hands and get the fuck out already.

The door shuts and she leaves. I grab my compact and flip it open and pour out a tiny rock and smash it and chop it and line it up and snort it. I snort it and it feels good. It hits my throat and stings. It stings and feels good. Fucking good. Fucking awesome. Fucking there. Fucking there, man. Yes.

I look at my watch. Fuck. I have ten minutes before I have to meet my lawyer. I gotta fucking go. Now.

I hop in my car and drive the couple of blocks to the courtroom. I park.

I see my lawyer pull up. I look in the rearview mirror and check to make sure there's no yellow powder in my nostrils. There's not.

I get out of the car and meet him. He says hello and asks me how I'm doing.

"I'm not good. I'm nervous and I'm afraid that I'm going to get into a lot of trouble."

He tells me it's normal to be nervous but with all of our evidence, he should be able to plea it down.

I tell him I'm scared. But okay.

We walk in the courtroom and go through the metal detectors and find a place to sit. We sit on a bench and he tells me he's going to go talk to the prosecutors. He gets up and walks over and I see him chat some small talk and I see him laughing and chuckling.

I sit and wait.

FLASH!
He holds out the breathalyzer.
I scream, "FUCK THAT! I WANT MY FUCKING ATTORNEY!"

FLASH!
I'm in the back of a cop car.
"DO YOU BELIEVE IN JESUS, YOU BALD-HEADED MOTHER FUCKER? BECAUSE YOU'RE GOING TO DIE! STUPID FUCKING PIGS!"

FLASH!
I'm handcuffed to the wall.
"I WANT MY FUCKING ATTORNEY! FUCK YOU ALL! IF YOU WERE REAL COPS YOU'D BE WORKING DOWNTOWN NOT OUT IN A FUCKING LAME SUBURB!"

FLASH!
I'm being un-cuffed from the wall.
"You're all just a bunch of fucking losers!" . . .

KNOCK. KNOCK. KNOCK.
Fuck. Court is now in session.
I sit and wait for my turn. I sit and dread going up in front of the judge. I wait and dread and know that my fucking life is over. It's fucking over. Over. Over. Over.
The City of Silk Hope vs. Me. Loser. Whore. Druggie.

My heart starts to beat faster than its present rabbit pace, and I feel like it's going to pop out of my chest. My hands start to sweat and tingle and I want to die. I want to fucking die. It's over. I'm fucking dead.

I stand up and my legs feel like Jell-O. They feel like they're going to collapse from underneath me. I feel lightheaded and like I'm going to pass out. I feel like I'm going to fucking pass out. Fucking pass the fuck out.

I don't hear anything but the sound of human voices in pieces.

". . . spoke to the prosecution . . . "

". . . struck a deal."

"Yes, we agreed."

". . . to plea . . ."

". . . lower sentence."

Miss Loser? Do you agree to the plea?

"Yes."

The word comes out because everyone is looking at me but I don't feel like I'm the one talking. I feel like I'm watching myself talk. My knees are shaking and my heart is pounding and my hands are wet and I'm scared. Scared and scared and scared.

I hear, Well, Miss Loser, it looks like the prosecution will agree to the plea. So your sentence has been reduced. Which is really sad for me, because I was really looking forward to reading your police report and hearing your response. It looked like a really good one.

The whole courtroom starts to laugh. Except for me. Miss Loser.

I'm humiliated and wish I could curl up into a ball and die.

Or do another line.

THIRTEEN YEARS OLD

We climb into the back seats of the truck cab and I watch my mom stumble into the driver's seat. Ramie and I look at each other and we know. We know because we do this all the time. We know because it's what we do every chance we get. I know because I've seen her like this so many fucking times it makes me want to fucking puke.

I'm nervous. I'm fucking nervous because she looks worse off than she should look to drive us home. I'm fucking nervous because I sat backstage and watched her.

FLASH!

We're at the high school in the theater. We're in the back with the models and clothes and hairstylists and makeup artists. Everyone's rushing about.

All of the makeup artists are passing around a bottle of booze. They're swigging straight out of the bottle. Ramie and I sit and watch and wish they would pass it to one of us. We sit and watch and fucking wish they would share the fucking bottle with us. They don't . . .

I look in the front seat of the truck as my mom struggles to get her seatbelt on. She's so fucking embarrassing. So fucking embarrassing. Whenever I'm around her I want to punch her in the face and then crawl into a fucking hole and drink a bottle of vodka. I fucking hate her. Fucking hate her.

I look at Ramie. She looks worried. She looks fucking worried because her parents don't drink. She looks worried because she doesn't want to die. She looks worried because her fate is in the hands of my idi-fucking-otic mother. My fucking alcoholic, white-trash mother's hands.

She tries to stick the keys in the ignition and starts to laugh with that stupid, fucking drunk laugh that she does when she's plastered. That annoying, obnoxious laugh that she gets when she's fucking wasted. She mumbles something to herself and finally the engine starts.

I look at Ramie and I know what she's thinking. She's thinking that my mother is a fucking disgusting loser and that I'm like her. She thinks that I'm like my mom. She thinks that I'm like my stupid fucking mom because I'm her daughter. She thinks I'm a fucking disgusting loser too.

I'm fucking embarrassed. I'm fucking embarrassed and feeling the RAGE take over me. I want to punch my fucking mom in the face. I want to kick her in the stomach. I want to rip her out of the car and stomp on her face. I fucking hate her! I want to fucking die and curl up and hide and all I feel is humiliation.

Humiliation. RAGE. Embarrassment. RAGE. Violence. RAGE. Hatred. I want to fucking hurt her and smack her and hide and tell Ramie she has to walk home. I want to fucking walk home. *I* want to fucking walk home.

My mom starts to drive and she's weaving all over the road. She crosses over the yellow lines and I look at Ramie. She looks nervous. Scared. Like she wants to fucking run. Jump out of the truck.

I know if I say something to my mom she isn't gonna like it. She's gonna get mad at me or ground me or something. I don't fucking care. I'm scared and angry and I want to beat the shit out of her for putting us in the truck with her when she's fucking wasted. She normally drives with her pink cup in the car with her, but this is fucking ridiculous.

"MOM, YOU'RE TOO DRUNK TO DRIVE. YOU'RE CROSSING OVER THE LINES."

"EHM FINE, ERBUHLUH. EH DINEVEN JRINK HARLY IINNYTHEEN EDALL."

I sit back in my seat. Fuck you! Fuck you, you fucking drunk bitch! I want to fucking scream at her. She doesn't even fucking care that we're in the back. That she's fucking wasted and her daughter and her daughter's best friend are in the back seat. I want to fucking die. I want to smash her face in. I want to fucking walk home.

And I'm fucking scared we're gonna get into a wreck. My heart starts to pound. Pound and pound and beat and beat with RAGE. It beats faster and faster and angrier and angrier.

Rage-rage. Rage-rage. Rage-rage. Ragerage. Ragerage. Ragerage. Rage-Rage-Rage-Rage-Rage-Rage-RAGE-Rage-RAGE-RAGE. The RAGE wants to split my chest open and grab her throat and squeeze the booze breath out of her.

We start to get into the curvy part of the road and I get more scared. I look at Ramie and she looks like she just saw a fucking ghost. She looks terrified. She looks terrified in her own Ramie way. She wants to fucking jump out of the truck.

FLASH!

My mom takes another swig of the booze as she packs her stuff up. My mom stumbles as she hands the bottle back to her co-worker.

Her co-worker looks at us and looks back at my mom and asks her if she's okay to drive home. She looks over at us and looks back at the co-worker and tells her she's fine. It's only like a fifteen-minute drive home. She's fine. She's hardly even got a buzz. She doesn't need to tell her that it's a five-mile drive of mostly ten-to-fifteen-mile-per-hour curves. All the roads are like that up here . . .

My heart is beating fast but now it's with terror. We approach a really sharp curve. My heart beats faster and faster and faster and I'm scared. She almost went into a ditch when the roads were practically straight and now we're going into the curviest part of the road.

Fuck. I'm fucking scared. I'm fucking scared and embarrassed and humiliated and wonder if Ramie thinks that I'm just like my mom. I wonder. I wonder and worry and fear and shame and embarrassment and RAGE and humiliation and violence.

We go into the curve and I see the headlights heading straight into the hillside instead of turning with the road. We're heading for the hillside and not the fucking road. We're driving too straight ahead and not turning with the road!

My heart pounds faster with fear and I look at Ramie. Her eyes are wide and I can see her breathing in the dark. I can see the fear trying to escape with each heave of her chest.

Suddenly the wheel yanks and we turn with the road and the two wheels on my side of the truck go into the ditch and then back out again.

Ramie gasps. My mom acts as if nothing happened.

My heart starts to pound with RAGE and fury and red fucking RAGE and I fucking lose it. I'm ready to rip her out of the fucking truck and leave her on the side of the road and try to fucking figure out how to drive the truck myself. I can do it. I've never done it, but I know I can fucking do a better goddamn job than this. I FUCKING HATE HER!!!

"MOM, PULL THE TRUCK OVER. YOU'RE GOING TO KILL US!"

She snaps back, slurring, "ERBUHLUH, EHM THU DULT HERE. YEW NEE DA SHUH DA HELLUP AN SIH INDA BACK. EHM FINE."

I'm seething with RAGE and I want to reach up and strangle the life from her itty-bitty, drunken bird neck. I want to squeeze and squeeze until there's nothing left.

"MOM! NO! I WON'T SHUT THE HELL UP! YOU ARE SO FUCKED UP AND YOU'RE GOING TO KILL US! PULL OVER AND LET ME DRIVE THE REST OF THE WAY HOME! PLEASE!"

She's pissed now and not paying as much attention to the road as she should be.

"DOE YEW SUH FFFUCK TUMMEE! EHM FINE. WUR AHMOSTOME. AN YER DA DAUGHER, NAH THE DULT. EHLL JIVEUS OME. EHM DA DULT, NAHYEW, ERBUHLUH!"

I look at Ramie and she can see the Rage welling in me. She can see the fucking RAGE and the desire and the temptation to smack my mom in the back of her head. She looks at me and tells me with her eyes that she wants to get out of the fucking truck and walk the rest of the way home.

I look at her and agree.

"MOM, WE HAVE A RIGHT TO RIDE HOME AND NOT GET KILLED. WILL YOU EITHER PULL OVER SO THAT WE CAN WALK HOME OR PULL OVER AND LET ME DRIVE? PLEASE!!!"

"NUH-WEY! SNOT SAAFE FERYEW TAWALK OME AHN THISCURVY ROADET NIGH. EN YEWDOE NOHOWTA JRIVE. FEW SAY NOTHER-FUCKIN WUR, YER GROUNED!"

That fucking does it. That fucking does it. The RAGE is streaming through my veins. The RAGE is streaming and beating and calling for me to rip her face off. Telling me to hurt her and not care. Telling me to punch her in the face. Punch and hit and smack and scratch and rage and Rage and RAGE.

"FUCK THAT, MOM! PULL THE FUCKING CAR OVER AND LET US OUT! YOU CAN DO WHATEVER YOU WANT WITH ME BUT YOU HAVE NO RIGHT TO DRIVE MY BEST FRIEND HOME WHILE YOU'RE FUCKING SLOBBERING FUCKING DRUNK! PLEASE PULL THE CAR OVER SO THAT WE CAN WALK! I'M BEGGING YOU!"

"NOWUNS SGETTE NOUT AHTHE CAR ERBUHLUH. AN WEH YEW GEH OME, YEW CACALL RAME'S PURNTS TA PIGGER UP CUZ YER-GROUNED FER UH MUNT. YEW JES DUNNO WHETA SHUDUP AN LEH ME BE THE DULT! EHM SOR RAME, BUH YERGUN AH HAVTA GO OME CUZ ERBUHLUH CANNA CUNTROL ER EGGER."

The passion has left her voice. She's in that place. That place where nothing I say matters. Yelling doesn't matter. Begging doesn't matter. And nice doesn't matter. None of it matters because she's being a bitch and it's her fucking way or the highway.

I sit and seethe. I seethe with RAGE and violence and fear and RAGE and pain and betrayal and embarrassment and punishment and bewilderment and humiliation and shame.

Shame and RAGE and humiliation rip through my veins. Shame and RAGE and humiliation. Shame. RAGE. Humiliation. RAGE. RAGE. RAGE. Rip. Rip. Rip.

I sit back and look at Ramie and see her fear. I feel my fear.

I feel my fear and pray that the swerving stops and we make it home alive.

TWELVE YEARS OLD

I look around the room. On the wall in front of me there's a life-size poster of a skinny, perfect, blonde model in a bikini. She's beautiful and I want to be her. I look down at my thighs and think how disgusting they are. I want to cut them into pieces. I want to cut the fat off and hurl it out the window. I want to hurl it out the window and be skinny like the perfect woman on the poster.

I am *fucking* disgusting. Fucking fat and disgusting. Why does this gorgeous guy want to de-virginize me? He's going to take one look at my fat and tell me how fucking sick and gross and disgusting I am.

I look over at the wall to my left.

I look over to my left and there's a clock. A handmade clock with one cardboard hand and a cardboard body. It's white with black writing. The hand is pointed where the three is supposed to be. But there's no three.

Instead of a three, there's a woman's name. All around the clock, there are different women's names.

12 o'clock: Jenny

1 o'clock: Kari

2 o'clock: Cara

3 o'clock: Linda

4 o'clock: Sara

5 o'clock: Amy

6 o'clock: Erin

7 o'clock: Dana

8 o'clock: Tracy

9 o'clock: Brittney

10 o'clock: Brenda

11 o'clock: Heather

I look at my thighs and see only fat. I see only fat and feel disgusting. I want to twist it and scream and rip it off. I'm furious. RAGEful. Vengeful. I am fat, fat, fat. Repulsive and disgusting. I want to cry and scream and stab my thighs with a pen or pencil or a razor or knife.

But I can't. I have to be quiet. I have to be quiet so that no one wakes up and hears me in here waiting for him. Waiting for him to come out of the bathroom and have sex with me.

Kim's cousin Brad is so gorgeous. Kim told me that for my first time I should have sex with him. She called me a week ago and told me that she had sex for the first time and that I should do it too. I should do it because it was so cool and I'm already twelve and it's time. It's time and her cousin is the perfect person. He's seventeen and gorgeous. She showed me his picture and he is. He's hot. Hot. Hot. Hot.

He's too hot for me. Why would he want to have sex with me? I'm twelve and ugly and fat and gross and nothing like the woman on the poster. I'm fat and ugly and disgusting and repulsive. I look at my thighs. I look at the fat blobs that are attached to my body and I get the sick feeling in my stomach and I want to scream and rip out my hair. RAGE and disgust and repulsion.

I want to lose my virginity. I want to lose my virginity to someone hot. No one knows that my cousin already had sex with me because then they would know that I had sex with my cousin and then they would think that I was disgusting and repulsive. They would know that I was a cousin-fucking whore. They would know that I was a slut. That I was a slut and then no one would want to come near me.

FLASH!

Matt is on top of me.

Matt is moving in and out and in and out.

Matt orders me to suck his dick.

I hate it. I hate sucking his dick.

I suck it and he pushes my head into it and shoves it down my throat.

I gag and suck and shame and shame and shame . . .

The door opens and Brad walks in. I shake my head and get the picture of Matt out of my head. I try to shake the shame and disgust off and I smile a tiny smile. A shy smile.

He whispers to me, "Hey, Arabella. You ready?"

I whisper back nervously, "Yeah, I'm ready."

I smile a little smile.

I'm scared because he's so big. He has no shirt on and his muscles are so big and perfect and hot and I'm just a disgusting little girl. He's a popular high school boy and I'm just a fat, gross girl who's friends with his cousin.

He comes up in front of me and grabs the bottom of my shirt and pulls it off.

My heart pounds with fear. Fear and shame. I don't want him to see my body. Not in the light. Not in the light. Not in the light. I don't want him to see my fat. My blobs. My tiny boobs. My fatness and grossness.

I whisper, "Can you turn off the lamp?"

He smiles.

"You don't want me to see you?"

I shrink and my heart pounds and I know that he knows.

"Not really."

He smiles.

"It doesn't matter to me. Light or dark, it's all the same to me."

He reaches over and dims the lamp.

I feel relief. Relief and fear and shame and panic. And my fat feels smaller. A little bit smaller. Now he can only feel it. Feel the disgustingness. He won't see the disgustingness. He'll only feel it. Feel it and maybe he'll be too busy screwing me to notice that I'm nothing like the girl in the poster. I'm nothing at all like her. I'm nothing compared to her. I am nothing.

He comes up to me and whispers in my ear, "Take your pants off."

I do what he says.

I take my pants off and he tells me to take off my underwear.

I do what he says.

He wraps his arms around my back and undoes the hook on my bra. My dad told me I don't need a bra. There's nothing there for a bra to hold up. I'm ashamed and feel disgusting and think of the perfect woman on the poster and I want to cover up my boobs. My M&Ms. My mosquito bites. My indentations.

He tells me to lie back on the bed.

I do what he says.

He climbs on top of me and starts to touch me with his fingers. He starts to bite my nipples and touch me in between my legs and stick his fingers inside of me.

He doesn't kiss me. He doesn't kiss me. He doesn't kiss me. I want him to kiss me. I want him to kiss me and I'll feel closer to him.

He looks at me. He must be reading my fucking mind. He whispers, "I don't kiss when I'm just fucking. I only kiss my girlfriend."

My heart sinks and my stomach starts to feel sick. I shrink into the bed. I sink into the bed and think how disgusting I am. I am repulsive. He's just fucking me. He doesn't want to kiss me because I'm not the skinny model on the poster. He doesn't want to kiss me because I'm fat and ugly. He doesn't want to kiss me because I'm not pretty enough. He doesn't want to kiss me because I am nothing.

He sticks his dick in me. He sticks his dick in me and moves in and out and in and out and I lay there. I move my legs up and lay quietly. I can't make any noise because his parents' bedroom is right above us.

I don't know if I would make any noise anyway. It would feel weird. With Matt I just do what he wants and stay quiet and wait until he's done. I feel like I do with Matt.

I just lay quiet and feel him go in and out of me. In and out and I shrink into the bed and think about my fat thighs.

He's thinking about my fat thighs. He's thinking that he wishes I was the woman in the poster. He wishes that I was pretty and skinny and blonde and something else. He wishes that my fat thighs were skinny and tan and long and smooth like hers.

He moves in and out and in and out and then he stops and whispers, "I want to eat out your little pussy."

I say okay.

I say okay but I shrink and feel disgusting. My stomach starts to twinge with shame and grossness and embarrassment and repulsion. My face is hot and uncomfortable and I want to shrink into the bed until I disappear. Disappear and shrink and go away. Away. Away. Away. Shrink. Smaller. And smaller.

I hate the word "pussy." I hate the word "pussy" and I hate the phrase "eating out pussy." Matt says that and it makes my stomach sick. It makes my stomach sick like it's sick right now.

He starts to lick between my legs and it feels good. It feels good because he uses his tongue to touch my spot. He flips it back and forth with his tongue and it feels really good. I'm getting hot and I'm throbbing down there now. I'm throbbing and my legs are getting shaky and I'm starting to feel turned on for the first time tonight. I'm hot and sweaty and throbbing and turned on.

I close my eyes and feel the throbbing and the good and try to push the picture of Matt out of my head. He flashes in and out and in and out. And in. He's in and I can't get him out. He's between my legs and I can't get him out. Can't get him out. Get out! Get out! Get fucking out!

"BBUUUUURRRRRRRGGGGHHHH!"

I hear a huge disgusting burp and feel breath blow on me down there.

Then he whispers a hissing, disgusting hissssssss.

"Sorry 'bout that, hon. Guess your little pussy is filling me up."

In the dark, I see his pronged tongue flip in and out of his mouth.

In and out.

In and out.

In and out.

TWENTY-THREE YEARS OLD

SMACK! SMACK! SMACK!

"You like that, baby, don't you? You're a fucking bad girl. A bad girl who needs to be beaten."

SMACK!

SMACK!

SMACK-SMACK!

I feel his smacks and his huge cock fucking me in and out and in and out and it hurts. It hurts because it's so big and because he's fucking me so hard. He pushes it in as far as it will go and I feel twinges in my uterus. It stabs deep inside of me. Deep and deeper, it hits the deepest part of me and it hurts.

My ass is starting to hurt. He's been spanking it for what seems like hours. It feels sore and blistered and hot and I need to roll over. I need to roll over but he's so into it. He's so into it that I don't know if he'll listen.

I tell him that I need to roll over because it's starting to hurt.

"That's the whole point, baby. You've been a bad girl and now I have to hurt you."

I raise my voice.

"I'm fucking serious, Joe! I need to roll over. I'm starting to hurt."

He says, "Oh, you think you can boss me around, huh?"

But he rolls me over onto my back while he says it.

"You're a bad fucking girl and you need to be punished with my huge cock."

He grabs underneath my legs and pulls me closer to him. He holds me underneath my knees and slides his cock back inside of me. He puts one leg down and uses that hand to start playing with me.

I stare up at him. I stare up at him as I lie on the mattress that's on the ground, as he moves in and out and in and out. The mattress lies on the ground like the one I had in my room. No one can grab me on his bed. No one but him.

He has a nice body. Muscular, lean, somewhat tan. He's hot. And he has a big fucking cock. He has a big cock and he doesn't care if I'm sleeping with other people. He's not one of those really jealous guys that always has to know what's going on and who I'm hanging out with. He doesn't care that I'm sleeping with the two other guys.

I'm hot and turned on. He touches me in between my legs and gets me nice and wet. He reaches up to kiss me. He's not a bad kisser. A little wet though.

I have fun with him. I have fun partying with him. We do "E" and drink and smoke weed and he's fun. There are always a lot of

Army guys at his house. But they're kind of off-limits. He's not jealous, but he doesn't want me fucking his friends.

I just want to have an orgasm and be fucking done with this. I want to be fucking done. God, let him get off. God, let me get off and be fucking done with this. Fucking done.

He whispers in my ear. Actually it's a hiss. He's fucking hissing disgusting things.

"I want to piss on you."

My heart pounds. I lose breath. What did he just say? What did he just fucking say? Did he actually ask me to let him fucking urinate on me?!?!

I push him forward, look into his snake eyes, and raise my voice.

"WHAT?!?!?"

"I want to piss on you because you've been a bad girl."

He's a snake. He's the predator and he wants his prey. He wants his fucking prey. He wants to squeeze the fucking life from me. He wants to squeeze it out. Constrict. Squeeze. Tighten. Kill. Suffocate.

"NO! NO FUCKING WAY, JOE! YOU'RE NOT FUCKING PISSING ON ME!"

He hisses more. I can actually see his little, pronged, red tongue dart out of his mouth as he speaks. Dart. Dart. Dart. Dart.

HISS.

HISS.

HISS.

"Oh come on, bad Bella. Let me piss on you. You're a bad girl and you need to be punished."

"I'M NOT FUCKING BEING PISSED ON, JOE! SO STOP FUCKING ASKING!! IT'S NOT GOING TO HAPPEN!"

He looks at me. He looks in my eyes. He looks at my eyes and his little, red, darting tongue slaps me on the chin as he stares. He needs something. He has to have prey. He has to dominate.

He has to constrict and squeeze and demean and control and dominate.

"Well, can I at least spit on your pussy?"

Oh my fucking God! He wants to spit on me. He wants to fucking spit on me. My heart beats faster and faster, like a rabbit. Thumping and pounding and my furry little chest is heaving up and down and up and down.

I want to scream, No! I want to scream, Get the fuck off of me! I want to scream, Get the fuck away, you fucking snake! I want to scream and wail and run and hide and hop into a dark hole and be safe. Safe and hide and breathe and safe and dark.

I say, "You want to spit on me?"

He hisses back, "Yeah, let me spit on my bad girl."

My heart beats faster. Bunny. I'm a fucking bunny. I'm a fucking bunny and I'm being squeezed. He's squeezing me. Tighter. Tighter. Tighter.

I won't let him piss on me. I won't let him piss on me so I should give him something. I should at least give him something. I should do what he wants. It's only for a minute. Who cares if I don't like it? It'll make him happy.

I should do it. I should just do it. I should just do what he wants and then he'll leave me alone. Constricting will stop. I'll breathe. Constricting and tightening and squeezing and then he'll release me. He'll get his life from me and then let me go. I'll be able to breathe again if I just let it happen and he'll go away and it'll stop and I'll breathe again.

I tell him okay.

He smiles. His eyes hiss and his smile hisses and his whole face hisses. He has his prey. He has his prey and now he gets to devour and squeeze and tighten and kill. And kill. And kill.

I watch him go down in between my legs. I feel the spit hit me. I feel the spit hit me once and I hear him hiss, "Bad girl. You're a bad girl."

I hear him hiss and I look at the ceiling and his hisses get quieter and quieter and quieter.

The spitting gets smaller and smaller and smaller.

I get smaller and smaller and smaller and smaller and smaller...

THREE TO FIVE YEARS OLD

"Look out the window at the rainbow, Arabella!"

I look at my babysitter. I cannot remember her name. But she's real nice to me.

"There is a rainbow out there?"

"Yeah, look out there . . ."

Oh, goodie. A rainbow. A rainbow. YAY! A rainbow! I love rainbows!

I pull myself up on the bed and I grab the sticks that go around the window. I grab the sticks and pull myself up and start to look out the window.

The sky is scary and grey like the walls down our stairs where my plastic kitchen is that I play in. The sky is scary and dark and I do not see the rainbow. Where is the rainbow?

WHACK! WHACK!

"OWIE!"

I cry out. I start to cry. Something hit my bottom. Something hit my bottom hard and it hurts. My bottom stings and stings and stings.

I let go of the sticks that go around the window and turn around to look at what hit me and my babysitter is smiling. She looks nice still, but my tummy feels icky. She looks nice but my tummy still feels icky.

"Why are you crying Arabella? Didn't you see the rainbow?"

I cry.

"I don't see no rainbow and something hit my bottom. Don't you see it? How my bottom got hit?"

"No. I didn't see anything. You must have been imagining it. Look out the window at the rainbow again and I'll see if I can see what hit you."

I look at her. I look at her and her teeth are showing and she looks nice. She looks nice and her teeth are showing. I look at her hands and she don't got nothing in them. I rub my bottom-hurt away.

She don't got nothing in her hands so I turn around. My tummy feels icky. I turn around and pull myself up on the sticks that go around the window.

I look at the dark, scary sky and see white lights and hear loud sky sounds. I look at the whole sky and don't see no rainbows. I look more.

WHACK! WHACK-WHACK!!

"OWIE! OWIE!"

I cry and fall onto the bed and turn around. My bottom hurts and something got me again. Something got me again.

I cry and look and her teeth are showing and she is holding that stick that my mommy uses to clean the floor. The one with the scare-crow on the end of it. She is holding it and her teeth are showing. And my bottom hurts and stings and she is looking real funny.

I cry and don't know what to do. I feel icky and scared and I want my mom. I want my mom. I want my mom. I want my mommy and I cry.

Her teeth are showing and she is holding the stick with the scare-crow on it. Her teeth are showing but my tummy feels icky cuz her eyes are little. Her eyes are little like she is a meanie. She is a meanie even though her teeth are showing.

Her eyes are little like a meanie kitty cat and I want my mommy.

SEVEN TO NINE YEARS OLD

House on Pine Road

I walk with my best friend over the bridge and down the road. We just got a bunch of candy at the Quick Stop. All sorts of candy. All sorts of colors and shapes and the wrappers are all shiny and noisy. I love candy.

We stand where the road goes to the left and where it goes to the right.

I ask Karen, "Do you want to walk to the left or to the right?"

She says, "There are mean dogs down that road. We should go the other way."

She points to the left.

I'm really scared of dogs that I don't know cuz I got bit by a Doberman Pinscher and cuz my mom is real afraid of them. So I like to take the road where there are no mean dogs.

We start walking and talking and thinking about all of our candy. On one side of the street there are houses and on the other is the river. It is really loud and sounds neat. I wish that my house was on the river.

I hear loud music and look over to one of the houses. The garage door is open and there is an old man staring at us. He is pretty old, not as old as my mom and dad but he is probably like twenty! He has long brown hair and he puts it in a ponytail like Karen's is.

He calls out to us.

"Hey you girls, how's it going?"

Me and Karen look at each other.

We both say, "Good."

We stand and talk to him for a while.

He sees me bite my nails and says, "You shouldn't bite your nails; when you have a boyfriend he'll want you to have long nails."

I ask him why.

He says, "So that you can scratch his back when you're playing with him."

My tummy feels weird because of the way he says that and because he kind of looks at me funny. That icky tummy meanness that I get when I am scared or real mad. But he is smiling at me and he seems really nice.

He asks us if he can walk us home. We look at each other. The tummy meanness is meaner and harder now.

I say, "No, we are fine."

He says, "Well, I can show you something really neat on the way back to your houses."

We look at each other again.

He is smiling. The tummy meanness is not as big now so I say, "Okay."

We walk nearer to our houses. When we get to the place in the road where Karen cuts off to go home, she says goodbye and that she will call me.

I tell her goodbye and I tell the old man goodbye too.

He says that he can walk me to my house because he still has not showed me what he wants to show me.

The tummy meanness is back. It feels funny.

"No, I'm fine," I say.

He says he wants to make sure that I get home okay.

So he walks me to my house.

My mom's truck is in the driveway but she is not home. There is a canopy on the back and he asks me if I want to get in the back of the truck with him and play a game. He says it will be really fun.

My tummy feels mean and twisty and funny but he is smiling and being nice and he seems real nice even though he is an old man.

I tell him okay.

We jump in the back of my mom's truck and he shuts the tail of the truck, but not the canopy window. He says, "We're going to play doctor. Do you want to be the doctor or the sick person?"

I say I will be the sick person.

I say that because I don't know how to be a doctor. I don't know what doctors are s'posta do. I know that I can act real sick cuz I have been real sick before. Like when I had a fire temperature and my mom and dad had to put me in the bathtub with icy water and lots of ice cubes. I know how to be sick real good.

He starts.

"Well, Miss Patient. What seems to be the problem?"

I look at him and think, He sure is a real nice old guy. He is playing a game with me. Dave does not ever do nice things with me. Or my mom or Bill. He is real nice.

"My ankle hurts, Doctor."

"Well, let's see what's going on here."

He grabs my leg around the bottom half, below where my knee is.

He picks it up and looks at it. I am wearing shorts. He says that he thinks that I hurt my leg up higher.

The tummy weirdness is back. The tummy weirdness is back but he is nice and he's playing a game with me. I should play the game with him cuz I said that I would and cuz he is older than me. He is an adult and I should do what he says.

I ask him, "Where did I hurt my leg up higher?"

He starts to grab me on my knee. Then his hand moves up above my knee and on the up half of my leg. Closer and closer to my privates.

My chest is beating fast and faster and harder and mean like my tummy. My tummy is tighter and meanness is coming and I feel funny and scared and weirdness. I feel icky tummy meanness. I don't want to play this game anymore. But he is an adult and he is nice and I am s'posta do what he says.

I hear a car pulling up and all of a sudden his hand jerks off of my leg. I turn around and my mom is pulling into the driveway.

I smile at her, but she does not look very happy. Then the old man starts to get out of the truck. As he gets out, my mom slams her car door and stomps up to him.

"WHO THE HELL ARE YOU?"

I see her talk but I don't hear what she said to him. After, I get into a lot of trouble for bringing a strange man home to the house. Mom says that I am grounded and she yells. She tells me how stupid I am cuz I let a strange man walk me home and get into the back of the truck. She tells me that she has told me a zillion times that I am not s'posta ever, ever let someone I don't know touch me. I see her really mad face as she talks to me. I feel like she doesn't love me. I feel like I am really stupid and wrong.

I feel like it's all my fault cuz I am a bad girl.

FOURTEEN YEARS OLD

"Arabella, have you been in my bedroom?"

I look at her. Oh shit. She knows.

"No, Mom."

"Are you sure? You haven't been snooping around my room?"

My heart starts to pound. She's gonna know. She's gonna know. Fuck. Fuck. Fuck. Keep cool. Keep cool. What's she gonna do? She can't tell me what's missing, cuz then I would know what she's been doing. Keep cool. Everything is fine.

"No, Mom. Geez. What's wrong?"

She looks nervous. Wound up. Uptight. Scared and worried. Confused. Should she tell me? Or not? I know that's what she's thinking.

She raises her voice. It's louder and more nervous and more scared and more accusing.

"ARE YOU SURE? SOMETHING IS MISSING FROM MY ROOM!"

I raise my voice back. The tone that says, Fuck, Mom, why are you asking *me*? I'm innocent. I swear. I have no idea what you're talking about.

But I really do.

"NO. I TOLD YOU I WASN'T IN YOUR ROOM. WHAT ARE YOU FREAKING OUT OVER? WHAT'S MISSING THAT'S SO IMPORTANT?"

She pauses. She looks at me and looks at the ground. She doesn't know what to do. She's confused and she doesn't know what to do or whether or not she should tell me.

She starts to look more nervous. She's more and more nervous. I know what she's missing because I took it. But she doesn't know that, and she can't tell me, because then she would have to tell me that she's doing something illegal. And she wouldn't do that because then I would know what she's been doing. And then she would be a big, fucking, fat hypocrite.

"I can't tell you what it was, Arabella. Do you swear that you didn't take anything from my room? Because Jim is missing something."

I look at her and really wish that she would fucking lay off. I wish that she would just lay off. I'm nervous. She's gonna know I'm lying if she keeps asking. She's gonna fucking know. My heart starts to beat faster and faster and thumps and pounds and beats and she's gonna see it pounding through my chest. She's gonna see my hands shaking and my eyes darting around, evading her.

"I swear, Mom. I swear that I didn't take anything from your room. I haven't even been in your room except to walk through it to get to the laundry room. What's Jim missing?"

Okay. That was good. Good lying. The laundry room thing helped. I don't normally lie very well, but that was perfect. She doesn't have a clue. That was a perfect fucking cover.

"I can't tell you what he's missing. But someone must have broken in the house and taken it. I already asked Dave and he said that he hasn't been in the room either. Have any of your friends been in the house when you were taking a shower?"

"No. I haven't had any friends over. And when I do, I don't take showers while they're here."

She's pacing now. She's pacing and nerving and worrying and thinking and getting more and more paranoid. This is fucking hilarious. She is fucking insane. A paranoid maniac.

She looks at me in my eyes. She looks to see if she can see the lies. She looks and searches with her stupid, fucking clown hair. She looks and searches and she won't find a thing. She searches long and hard.

I just look at her. It's a stand-off. My eyes say I'm innocent. My eyes say my friends are innocent. My eyes say you're a fucking idiot. My eyes say move on to the next idea. My eyes say move on because you're not getting anything from me. I will never confess.

She paces. She's like the mountain lions at the zoo. The ones that pace back and forth and back and forth in their cages. They pace and look for relief that they'll never find. She's one of them. Pacing and searching.

God, she's fucking paranoid, thinking my fucking friends are gonna ransack her room. This is unfuckingbelievable. This is a joke. She's a fucking joke. I just want her to break down and tell me what's missing. I want her to break down and tell me what's missing and humiliate herself. I want her to be humiliated. Fucking humiliated.

She looks and thinks. I can tell that she's thinking about whether or not she should tell me. Whether or not she should fucking tell me that she's doing illegal things that could get her kids taken away from her. I wait and watch her think. I can see the little gerbil wheel spinning in her head. Should I or shouldn't I? Hmmmmm.

It's not as if it's not totally fucking obvious. Does she think that we're that fucking stupid? They blocked off the basement windows with plywood. The door is barricaded. There's light coming out from the edges of the plywood.

There was no light there before she started to see Jim. There was no plywood and no padlocked door. She must think we're fucking morons. Seriously. Fucking morons.

She paces more and more and the smoke shoots out of her ears. There's smoke shooting out of her ears from where her brain is supposed to be. There is smoke shooting out from where her brain is supposed to be. It's fucking hilarious.

She looks at me and I can tell she's gonna say something.

I interrupt. I interrupt just to fuck with her. To see more smoke and more pacing.

"Maybe you should call the cops. If you think someone broke into the house you should probably call the cops, Mom. I think you should call the cops. Now you got me scared."

She stops and looks at me. There's a terror in her eyes. She's fucking scared. She doesn't know what to do. She's backed into a corner and now she has to tell me. HA! HA-HA! This is fucking great! Fucking great!

She takes a deep breath.

"Arabella, I have to tell you something."

I play the worried daughter. The scared girl who wants to know what her mother is talking about.

"What, Mom?"

"If I tell you, you can't tell anyone, okay?"

I say okay. But I think, Yeah, sure. Right. I'm not going to tell anyone.

"You know that Jim smokes pot, right?"

"Uh, I figured as much. His eyes are always beet red and he smiles all the time."

"Well, he wanted to do something here. I told him that he couldn't and I didn't want him to. But I let him talk me into it."

Oh God, here she goes. Playing the poor little victim whose boyfriends *make* her do things that she doesn't want to do.

"Well, he's been selling drugs out of the house."

I act really surprised.

"Really? He's selling drugs? No way!"

"Yes. That's why the basement is closed off. He's growing pot down there."

I act even more surprised.

"He's growing pot?!?! Mom, that's illegal. You could go to jail for growing pot in the house."

Her face looks ashamed and guilty and humiliated. Now I don't really want to see her feel that way. I feel sorry for her. I feel bad for even wanting her to feel that way. She's just a pathetic little girl. I look at her and see a pathetic, weak woman who does whatever her men want her to do. Even if it goes against what she knows in her heart to be right.

"I know it's illegal. That's why you can't tell anyone."

I tell her okay. I ask her if that's what was missing from the bedroom. I know it isn't. But, I have to play stupid.

"No, that wasn't what was in there. It was worse. That's another reason why I can't call the cops."

I still play stupid. Not to humiliate her this time. I still feel sorry for her. Just to cover my ass.

"What, Mom? Was it cocaine or something?"

"No. I told him I didn't want to do it. I told him that the pot was going far enough. But he thought that we could make more money this way."

"What is it, Mom?"

"You can't tell anyone, okay?"

"I won't. Tell me."

"Mushrooms. He is selling mushrooms and they were under the dresser with a scale and now half of them are missing."

My heart starts to beat. Fuck. Fuck. I can't let her see my guilt. I have to stay calm and cover my fear and act surprised. Act fucking surprised, Arabella. Fucking surprised. Do it. You must do it. Survival mode. Survival mode. Survival Mode.

"Really? Mushrooms? You hate drugs, though."

"I know, I know. I shouldn't have let him do it. But now I'm worried that someone knows. Someone must've broken into the house. I'm worried and scared and I know I shouldn't have done it. Now I have to tell him to get rid of it all and I don't know what to do."

I feel bad. I listen to her go on and on and I feel bad for her. I feel bad that she's scared. I feel bad that she doesn't know what to do. I feel bad that she's so paranoid that she thinks that there's someone breaking into the house to steal her drugs. I feel bad that me and Ramie took the mushrooms last weekend and had a great trip.

I feel bad that she's scared. But I can't tell her. I'll get into too much trouble.

I feel bad. But I have to put myself first.

I have to put myself first like she has put herself first my entire life.

She'll live.

TWELVE YEARS OLD

I sit down at the dining room table. My brother sits across from me.

My mom stares at us. She suspects. She condemns. She accuses. She convicts. We're already convicted so it doesn't matter what we say.

"I know one of you stole my cigarettes."

She eyeballs us. She waits for an answer.

I look at Dave. He looks at me. We look at each other and wait for the other to confess.

I speak first.

"I didn't take anything from you, Mom. I didn't take your cigarettes. I swear."

I tell her this honestly. I didn't take her cigarettes. I don't even know where she keeps them. I wouldn't even know where to look. So my brother better confess because I know that *I* didn't take them. He had to have taken them. I know he took them because I didn't take them.

He looks at me.

He looks at her. He speaks.

"I didn't take 'em Mom. I swear. I think Arabella took 'em."

"WHAT? I didn't take your cigarettes, Mom! He's lying!"

I want to smack his stupid-ass face. I didn't fucking take the cigarettes and he's trying to pin it on me. And she'll probably believe him because he's older. And he's a good liar. I'm not.

"Well, one of you took them. Cigarettes don't just get up and walk away. I know one of you took them. So you both get to go to your rooms and you're going to stay there until one of you decides to come clean about who took them. You know how much I hate lying. You both know how wrong it is. So you're both grounded until the person who took them comes clean."

I feel like someone smacked me. I feel the RAGE. It's welling in me. I want to fucking jump over the table and choke my brother for lying. I want to punch my mom in the face for accusing me and not looking me in the eyes and believing me. For not knowing when I am telling her the truth.

It's always the fucking same with her. She never believes me when I'm telling her the truth. She thinks that I'm a fucking liar. I fucking hate her. I hate her. I hate this house. I hate my brother. I hate my dad. I hate my white-trash family. I hate this shit-filled life and I want to die.

I speak. I beg.

"Mom, I swear that I didn't take them. Dave's lying. He's lying. I know because I know for a fact that *I* didn't take them, so it had to be him. Don't you believe me? I swear."

Dave pipes up.

"No, Mom. She's lying. I didn't take them. I hate smoking. Why would I take them? Arabella's lying."

He looks at me with that disgusting, fucking, I'm-going-to-get-you-in-trouble-and-I-don't-care-if-you're-innocent look.

"You know you took 'em, Arabella. Why don't you just admit it?"

I scream. My heart pumps and I want to strangle him.

"I DIDN'T TAKE HER CIGARETTES! YOU'RE LYING AND YOU KNOW YOU ARE BECAUSE YOU KNOW THAT I DIDN'T TAKE THEM!!!"

My mom interrupts us.

"Both of you get to go to your rooms now. And when one of you is ready to confess, then the person who didn't take them will be ungrounded. But until that time, you are both grounded. Go to your rooms."

I look at Dave. I stare at him with the most evil look that I can twist my face into. I want to sear his heart with hateful rays from my eyes. I want to strike him down with my RAGE. I want to fucking kill him. I know I'm not lying. I know that I didn't take the cigarettes. So I know that *he* did. I fucking hate him.

He walks up behind me as I go to my room. He taunts me.

"Why don't you just admit that you took them, Arabella? You know that you did."

I turn around and want to smack him across the room. Fucking pound his face in. Kick him down the stairs. Hurt him. Hurt him for all the times he's hurt me. Kick his stupid, buck-toothed ass. His stupid, buck-toothed, zit-faced ass. Kick him down the stairs.

I think about it. I could do it. I'm in reach. He's at the edge of the top of the stairs.

But I don't.

Instead, I go to my room and I marinate in RAGE. I marinate in it and feel it and swear and cuss and think about how much I hate my stupid fucking family. I get out my journal. I get out my journal and I write.

On one page:

I HATE MY MOM!

On the next page:

I HATE MY BROTHER!

On the next page:

I HATE MY DAD!

On the next page:

I HATE MY LIFE!

On the next page:

NO ONE EVER BELIEVES ME!

TWENTY-NINE YEARS OLD

Hope is dead.

I am dead.

Who is this woman staring back at me?

Who is this woman?

Maybe I just need to accept the fact that I'll never be what I dream of being. That I'm just filled with too much shit and pain to overcome all of this and help the world the way I want to help it.

Who wants to hear about some fucked-up, depressed woman who can't live life like everyone else? Who wants to hear about all the bullshit that happened to her growing up?

And so the RAGE sets in.

This is just a waste of fucking time. You can't even pull yourself out of bed half the time. What makes you think that you're going to help anyone else?

Seriously. You actually think that there's something about you that makes you special? That there's something about you that will help people? You think there's something about you that people will be affected by?

Gimme a fucking break. You are nothing. Nothing. You'll probably end up alone, alone for the rest of your life. All alone and crying and wishing that you had something special to give to the world.

Face it, Arabella. These are all just wishes. Plenty of other people grow up in abusive homes. Plenty of people are punched by their fathers and brothers and fucked by their cousins and thrown to the wolves by their mothers. And plenty of these people turn their lives around and create something better for themselves.

So you're writing a book. But look at you. Look at you! FUCKING LOOK AT YOU! You can't even function without being on antidepressants. You can't even pull your ass out of bed without the help of pills.

Face it. Just fucking face it now. You're a weak person who has to depend on medication. Just like you were a weak person when you were doing drugs. Just like you were a weak person when you were binge eating.

You are weak. It's never going to change. You might as well end it now. Just fucking do it. Put yourself out of your misery.

Oh, but you're too much of a coward to do it, aren't you? You think because your boyfriend betrayed you and your mother and father abandoned you that you have something to hold onto.

Let me tell you something. You have nothing. You will never amount to anything.

Keep writing all you want. It won't do you any good because you aren't one of those people that things come to. You're not. You're fucking not.

FUCK YOU, VOICES!!

Yes I am.

Yes I am.

Yes I am.

Yes I am.

Yes I am.

Please God, tell me that I AM.

TWENTY-NINE YEARS OLD

(Day One, 6:09 p.m.)

I stand on the deck and feel like pulling all of my hair out. I feel like pulling handfuls of fucking hair out as I wait. Each minute is an eternity. An eternity of swirling confusion. An eternity of unanswered questions. An eternity of betrayal. An eternity of lies and deception and of my life not making any sense. An eternity that my life is a fucking nightmare come true.

I try to take deep breaths. I try to take deep breaths as I suck down cigarette after cigarette. I wait and itch and feel my heart racing. Pounding. Thumping. Threatening to crush my ribs as it bursts out of my chest.

I wait. I wait. I wait.

I wait and feel my stomach turn. I feel my intestines twisting. Wrenching. Squeezing. Wringing. The twisting wants to run up my throat and out of my mouth, but I swallow it with the squeezing and think about taking deep breaths.

Then I hear them. Motorcycles. Motorcycles from far away. He's coming. He's fucking coming. My stomach turns and twists and my heart starts to beat faster and faster and harder and harder. My hands start to shake. I feel the adrenaline rushing through my veins. Pumping. Pumping. Pumping. Pumping. I'm speeding up. I feel like I'm going to explode. I'm going to fucking explode. Fucking explode!

I look off of the deck and see the motorcycles turn onto the road. I see him. I see him and I want to fucking explode.

FLASH!
"I looked in the box and found *it*."
SMACK!
"*It's* not mine. I'm holding *it* for Jon."
SMACK! SMACK!! . . .

I stand on the deck and feel the RAGE growing. And growing. And taking over my body. I'm shaking like I've never shaken before. Quaking. Trembling. Unstable.

I hear the front door open. I hear the front door open and I hear all of his friends come in. I want to fucking kill all of them. Just the whispers of their male voices make me want to jump up and strangle each and every last one of them. I hate them all. Every last one of them.

I stay on the deck and feel my heart pumping through my chest. Pump. Thud. Thump. Pound. Pound. Crush. Crush. Crushing my ribcage with every thud.

I stare at the road and feel as if the thumping of my heart could throw me over the banister and off the deck and smash me onto the concrete trail below.

"Bella?"

I stare at the road. I don't answer.

"Bella, these guys are just getting some of their riding gear and then they're leaving and we can talk, okay?"

His voice is too nice. It's a sweet and gentle voice. It's a kind voice. I've heard that kind of voice before. It's the voice of a guilty person. The voice of someone who knows they've fucked up. The voice of someone who has betrayed you.

The voice of my mom.

SEVENTEEN YEARS OLD

I touch my hair. I grab a velvety-soft, auburn strand between my fingers. It's so much softer than I've ever felt it. I look at it. I stare at the deep auburn color.

I am never going to touch my hair again. Never.

What have I done?!?! I'm never going to touch my hair again.

FLASH!

BANG! BANG! BANG!

My door bursts open and there are paramedics everywhere. I lie in the bed and wonder what's going on. I see Ellie. I see men everywhere. Men everywhere.

One of them leans down near me. Pulls me up to a sitting position.

I hear the mumbling of a name and that he works for the fire department and then he asks me how many pills I took.

"I dunno."

What day of the week is it?

"Tuesday."

It's not Tuesday, though. It's another day of the week . . .

I stare down at my hair and think about what I've done. I lie in the ambulance and all I can think is that I'm never going to touch my hair again. I'm never going to touch my hair. Then I hear voices behind me. I hear voices right behind me! Who is that? Who's talking? It's so loud. So very loud.

I ask the paramedic.

"Who's talking behind me?"

He stares at me and tells me that no one is behind me. We're in an ambulance. There's only a wall behind me.

Then he looks at me with kindness and asks me why I did it.

I can't tell him. I can't tell him cuz no one knows. No one can ever know. I can't tell him, so I say I don't know; I just don't want to be alive.

FLASH!

"Okay, Arabella. I'm going to help you stand up and we're going to walk you to the ambulance right outside. Can you do that?"

I say yes but all I can think is that I don't have a bra on. I don't have a bra on and all of these hospital people and firemen are going to see me without a bra. They're going to cut my shirt open and see me without a bra and laugh. I have to get a bra on. I have to get a bra on. I have to get a bra on.

He helps me stand and I tell him that I have to grab something out of my dresser. Somehow I grab it and as he walks me down the hall I bolt into the bathroom and lock the door.

I hear panicky screaming.

"WHAT ARE YOU DOING IN THERE? WE'RE BREAKING THE DOOR DOWN IF YOU DON'T COME OUT RIGHT NOW!"

I yell back that I'm just going to the bathroom. I don't know why I don't just tell them that I need to get my bra on. But I don't.

As I fasten the last clasp of the bra and pull down my shirt the door flies open. Paramedics everywhere. Everywhere. Rush. Bodies rush everywhere. Men and paramedics rush in.

Two of them take me by my arms and help me out of the bathroom to make sure that I don't finish the job with the razor in the shower . . .

I stare at the IV in my arm and feel the rush of the ambulance. I still hear the voices behind me. I still hear the voices and there's no one there. I grab a piece of my extra-velvety hair and as I do I start to feel my stomach turn. I start to feel my mouth water. I start to feel like I'm gonna—

RETCH.

VOMIT.

"AGGGHHHHH . . ."

My stomach contracts and squeezes and forces the acid and pills up my throat and out my mouth.

"AAAAAAGGGHHHHH . . ."

All I taste is acidy pills. Acid and pills. Sour, nasty pills and acid. I smell a stench. I smell a stench and taste the stench and feel the stench in my body. In every limb. Every fiber of my being is stench and poison and pills and acid. I cry.

I look at my hair and cry. I look at my hair and wonder what I've done. I look at my hair and think of God and wonder when I will see Him. I wonder and I start to hear voices.

"I love you, Arabella."

"You are so sweet."

"You are so pretty."

"I love you. I love you. I love you."

I hear voices and love. I wonder where they are coming from. I look out the back of the ambulance windows.

Oh my God! There are tons of faces staring into the windows! There's another ambulance attached to the back of this one!

Oh my God! It's holding everyone who's close to me. I see all of their faces pressed up against the window. Pressed up and looking in at me and smiling. I see love in their eyes.

I'm in a sea of loving words echoing through the ambulance and everyone that I've ever cared about during my life is staring into the ambulance and telling me they love me without their lips moving.

Nothing is real. Nothing is real except for the voices of love and the faces and the thought that I will never touch my hair again.

I will never touch my hair again.

I will never touch my hair again.

I will never touch my hair again . . .

TWENTY-NINE YEARS OLD
(Day One, 6:16 p.m.)

He steps out onto the deck. I don't look at him. I stare off of the deck at the cars passing by. I can't. I can't look at him. He has stolen everything I know and thrown it away. He's crushed what I think is real. Everything that I knew to be true—what I thought was real—he has crushed. He's taken my heart and stomped on it. So I can't look at him.

He tells me he's only been doing *it* for the past few months. He tells me he started doing *it* because of all of our sexual problems resulting from the sexual abuse that I endured growing up. It's all my fault. He started to do *it* to deal with our problems in the relationship. He did *it* to deal with all of the feelings that he had about me having issues with sex.

RAGE is constant in me. It's overtaken me. It is me. It pulses through my veins. My skin. My being. He's blaming me. It is all my fault. It was all my fault. In the beginning of our relationship I told him that I would leave him if I found out that he was using. He couldn't come to me. *It's* all my fault.

He did nothing wrong. He can't help it. He can't help it. He can't help it. *It* was all he knew how to do.

Everything is blurry. Everything is blurry and floating and his mouth is forming words and I'm listening, but nothing is real. Everything feels like a nightmare. Like the nightmares that I've been having throughout our whole relationship. The nightmares that led me to this moment, the ones that now define this moment.

I feel dizzy. I feel surges of RAGE. With every word I'm being hurled into emotions that I didn't know existed.

I'm out of control. I'm in utter shock. I'm in utter disbelief. I'm in utter denial. I'm in utter RAGE. I'm in utter horror. I'm in utter dismay. I'm in utter grief. I am in utter—

SNAP!

There is no reality. Everything that exists is surreal. I am in the nowhere that I have been before. It is a nowhere that I recognize. How did I get here? How do I get out?

I don't know who I am. I don't know who he is. I don't understand anything.

Someone please help me.

TWENTY-NINE YEARS OLD

(Day Two, 9:31 a.m.)

BEEP. BEEP. BEEP. BEEP. BEEP. BEEP.

I roll over and slam my hand on top of the alarm. The beeping stops. And I start to cry. I start to cry because I know that the nightmare I just had is warning me of what is to come.

Even though throughout our whole relationship I've had dreams that he was doing things to hurt me, I passed them off as my subconscious fears. I'd wake up and tell him and he would hold me in his arms and tell me that none of it was true. But the dreams became more frequent and more intense. And more real.

And now I know that those dreams, like the one I just had, are more than just subconscious fears. I can't ignore them any longer. They've moved out of my mind and into my life in a very real and concrete way. My fears have been realized.

FLASH!

"You've got to be kidding me? This is all *my* fault?!?!? Because you can't be by my side and help me through my intimacy issues around sex, you are actually blaming *me* for going out and doing what *you've* done? Do you even want to stop?"

"Not really."

SMACK!

"Not really?!?!?" . . .

I stare at the alarm clock and cry. I feel as though someone's scraped everything out of my heart with a razor blade. I feel like someone's stood above me and stomped on my stomach until it burst open. I feel pain like I have never felt.

I have never trusted anyone. Never. I never could. I never learned how to. I never had anyone give me any reason to trust them. Never ever in a relationship with a man have I been able to trust. Not even in a relationship with a man I *thought* I trusted. The sad thing is, at the time, I didn't think that I *did* trust him. But I didn't realize that until my trust had been broken.

I lie in bed and stare at the alarm clock and wonder if I can get out of bed. I don't think that I can ever get out of bed again. I think about my dream.

He cheated on me and lied to me and he didn't tell me everything.

There was more.

I cry and know that my dream is true. I know that he's not telling me the something more. Then I question myself. Am I going crazy? Maybe I'm just more scared now because I found out that he was lying to me and so I'm thinking there's more. Maybe he's telling me the whole truth. But there was the dream. I get the feeling there's more. But I can't trust my feelings, because I trusted them with him and I was wrong.

I'm spinning. My head is spinning and thinking and thinking and thinking and crazy and crazier and I'm losing my mind. I'm going crazy. I am going crazy.

Somehow I get out of bed and the rest of the day is a blur. I know that I call him more than once and he doesn't answer. I know that I go over to the house in the afternoon and find him sleeping. I know that I stand above him with my arms crossed wondering if he was getting fucked up the previous night. I know that he tells me that he was just sleeping. I know that I don't believe him.

I know that I take a shower. I know that I clean the litter box. I know that I don't eat. I don't eat a bite. I feed myself only nicotine and caffeine. The day is a blur of dizzy, crazed time passing more slowly than it has ever passed in my life. I'm sucking down cigarettes and coffee and shock.

He shows up later that night. He shows up and tells me that he found something special for me. He whips out a Dane Cook CD. He's my favorite comedian. Now I *know* that there's something more. He's buttering me up. Even through the shock and the sickness and the haze of unreality I can see that.

I take a deep breath and brace myself for more.

He says, "I have to tell you something."

I say okay.

He tells me that he's afraid that I'm going to leave him if he tells me.

I say, "Just tell me. Please."

He takes a deep breath. He takes another and another and as he breathes I feel my heart race faster and faster and my stomach get sicker and sicker and I brace myself. I try to prepare.

He starts.

"I haven't been doing *it* for only the past few months."

My eyes widen and I brace myself. My heart races and I feel my jaw tightening. Tighter and tighter and tighter. I want to fucking knock him out. I want to scream. I want to run. I want to jump. I want to die.

"I've been doing *it* since about six months into our relationship."

"WHAT?!?!? YOU'VE BEEN DOING *IT* FOR A YEAR AND A FUCKING HALF?!?!?! OH MY FUCKING GOD!?!?!?"

My head starts to spin and I start to get sick. I feel like I'm going to fucking hurl. I feel like I'm going to pass out. I start thinking about all of the lies. I get visions of when he said he was here or there and doing this or that and he was really somewhere else. Doing something else. All of the conversations. All of the fucking conversations. All of the fucking lies. All of the hundreds, even thousands, of fucking lies.

My head is spinning. I am spinning in a world that I can't make any sense of.

Our whole relationship has been a lie.

TWENTY-NINE YEARS OLD
(Day Three, 7:47 a.m.)

I awake from another nightmare. My heart is pounding and I feel sick and I want to die because I know that the nightmare is reality. He cheats on me in the dream. He cheats on me and doesn't care. He tells me that he doesn't want to be with me. He tells me that he's happy with someone else.

I don't know if it's true. I don't think it can be true. I don't want it to be true. Please, God, don't let it be true. Don't let him have cheated on me. Please. Please. Please.

Don't I deserve anything after all that I've been through?!?! Don't I at least deserve someone who will love me? Someone who I can trust? Someone who I can count on?

What's happening? I don't understand this. God, I don't fucking understand this. How's this happening to me? *Why* is this happening to me? It doesn't make any sense. He told me that he loved me and that he was sober and now I find out he's been lying to me for our whole relationship.

Then I get this surge through my body. It hits me as if someone has smacked me in the head with a frying pan.

WHACK!

He's not telling you all of it. He's not telling you everything. There's more.

Oh fuck you, you goddamn voices! I'm sick of your paranoia. Go away! GO THE FUCK AWAY!!!

The phone rings. He wants to come over.

Fuck! Fuck! Fuck! He's coming over to tell me something. He needs to tell me something more. I fucking know it! I fucking know it! I just know it.

I wait and pace and pace and pull my hair out and pace and breathe and can't breathe and think and suspect and wonder what else he's going to say. He fucking cheated on me. I bet he fucking cheated on me. Oh God, what if he cheated on me? I don't think I could take it. I know I couldn't take it. I'll die. If he cheated on me, I'll die. I will fucking die. Fucking die.

I sit outside and smoke cigarette after cigarette after cigarette and feel my heart beat faster and faster until it feels as if it will burst out of my chest. I try to think and I can't anymore. Every time a thought pops into my mind, dread takes over my whole body. All I feel is dread and doom and hurt and Rage and bewilderment. I can only think, How did this happen? How did this happen? How could this possibly be happening?

Over and over and over. How did this happen?

I hear his truck pull up and I go inside. I sit on my glider and feel my body tighten. I feel my body tighten and I feel my heart start to run faster. Race. Adrenaline surges through my head. I feel each pore on my face and each follicle on my head start to ache and hold its breath.

I hold my breath.

I exxxxhhhhhaaaaalllllleeeeee.

I hear his footsteps on my deck.

CLOMP.

CLOMP.

CLOMP.

CLOMP.

I want to run and hide. I want the angels to come take me away. I want to wake up. I want all of this to be a dream. A bad dream. I want to wake up and realize that he is who I thought he was. I want it to be a week ago. I want it to be a week ago because that's when my life made sense.

The door opens and I look up at him.

He looks at me.

He looks guilty. Fuck! He *is* going to tell me something! He looks like he knows something that I don't. He looks like he's scared.

Good! I hope he's fucking scared! He deserves to feel what I've felt like for the past three days. For my whole life! My whole fucking life I've been scared!

He sits down on the floor in front of me.

"Hey."

"Hey."

"I have to tell you something."

I look at him. I can't feel anything. I'm numb. All except my heart. All I feel is my heart racing. Pumping. Running. Waiting. Breaking. Breaking. Breaking.

"What?"

He takes a deep breath.

Déjà vu. Déjà fucking vu. When is this going to fucking stop?!?!?!? When is this going to end? When is my life going to make sense again?

"What I have to say is really hard for me. I'm really scared that you're going to leave me. I really need to tell you this because I need to be honest with you, but I'm really afraid that you're going to leave me."

"DID YOU CHEAT ON ME?"

"No. I didn't cheat on you. I didn't."

"What then?"

My heart doesn't slow down. I don't feel any better than I did before he answered the question because I don't believe anything that he's going to tell me. He's a goddamn liar. A fucking liar. A heartless fucking liar! He's probably lied a thousand times so far. How many conversations we've had about how glad we were to be sober. How life is great without it. How he would tell me if he were to do anything. It was all fucking lies. Lies. Lies. Lies.

He takes a deep breath and starts to tell me more.

"I'm going to come clean with everything, okay?"

"EVERYTHING? HOW MUCH MORE IS THERE?"

"I need you to stay calm so I can spit this out. I need you to stay calm. This is really hard for me."

I take a deep breath and feel my face tingle. It tingles like it did when I used to hyperventilate for fun. My hands tingle and my feet tingle and my face tingles and my heart breaks. Cracks. Splits. Bleeds.

He takes another deep breath and he starts.

"Remember when you asked me to get rid of my porn at the beginning of our relationship?"

"YEEEEAAAAH?"

I feel rage welling inside of me. I want to explode. I want to fucking explode.

"Well, I told you that I gave it to my brother, but I really didn't. I kept it for a few months. I just wasn't ready to get rid of it."

SMACK.

"YOU WEREN'T *READY* TO GET RID OF IT?!?!?!? WHAT?!?! ARE YOU KIDDING? YOU TOLD ME THAT YOU GOT RID OF IT! YOU LIED FOR OUR WHOLE RELATIONSHIP!!!"

His voice shakes. His voice shakes and my Rage wells. RAGE surges.

"I know. I know. I know that I lied. I was scared. I was scared to tell you the truth. You told me that you hate it when men watch porn. You told me that you wouldn't be with me if I had it."

"THAT'S BECAUSE I DIDN'T WANT TO BE WITH SOMEONE WHO WAS A FUCKING PIG!!!! YOU KNOW HOW I FEEL ABOUT THAT SHIT. YOU KNOW THAT I CAN'T FUCKING STAND IT!"

"I'm not a pig! I have a problem. I need help."

"YOU NEED HELP?!? YOU NEED FUCKING HELP?!?! WHAT DO YOU NEED FUCKING HELP FOR?!?!"

"You need to calm down so that I can tell you, okay?"

"NO, YOU NEED TO JUST TELL ME!"

"Okay."

He takes another deep breath. As he breathes in, I feel more and more of my soul being sucked into his lungs. More and more of me is swallowed into him. More and more of me disappears.

He continues.

"You know how I told you that Jon was looking up porn on the Internet?"

My heart starts to beat. It's going to explode. Implode. Self-destruct. I have to run. I can't hear what I'm about to hear. Must run. Must hide. Must get out and run!

I just say, "Yeeaaahh?"

"Well, I have a problem. I've been looking at porn on the Internet."

SMACK-SMACK.

"WHAT?"

I can't stand it anymore. My worst fear. My worst fucking fear. My worst fucking fear. FUUUUUUUCKKKKKKKKK!

My boyfriend lies. My boyfriend is a pig. My boyfriend lusts after and objectifies other women. The man that I've been making love to for the past two years has been cheating on me with sluts on the Internet.

"There's more, Bella."

SMACK-SMACK-SMACK-SMACK-SMACK-SMACK!

"THERE'S MORE? ARE YOU KIDDING ME?"

"No, I have to tell you everything. I want to come clean and be honest with you. You said that if there was any chance of this working out between us that I need to tell you the whole truth. Okay?"

Nothing is real. I just found out that my worst fear has happened and is happening. My boyfriend is a pig. My boyfriend masturbates to other women. My boyfriend's been lying to me. My boyfriend is someone else when I'm not around. My worst fucking fear.

I want to scream. Every aching fiber of what's left of my being wants to scream AAAAAAAAAAHHHHHHHHHHHHHHH!!!!!!!!

But I don't. Instead I say, "Okay. Tell me all of the truth."

I take a deep breath and wait for my fate. I wait for the end of the world. I wait for the world to be placed on my shoulders. I wait for that weight to crush what's left of me.

I wait with breath that is baited.

He takes a deep breath and another deep breath. I breathe in with him. I breathe in with him and disappear into his words. Into the crushing, deafening truth of what he tells me.

"I've been, uh, looking up porn on the, uh, Internet and . . ."

He takes another deep breath. As he does my head starts to spin and everything's getting whirly and dizzy and more unreal—if that's possible. I don't say anything. I have no words left. I am falling further and further into a black hole. A black hole. A dark, suffocating black hole that has stolen what is real, what makes sense, who I know, what I know, everything that was true.

As I fall farther into the depths, he continues.

"Patrick gave me some porno magazines. I've been doing it off and on for most of our relationship. But especially since all of the sexual abuse stuff has come up in therapy. I'm addicted to it. I need help. I can't stop."

I stare at him and as I do I see that pathetic-little-child look that my mom gets. That look that says, Feel sorry for me, I can't help what I do. It's not my fault. I'm a victim. Put your feelings aside and take care of me because I'm the real victim here. Feel sorry for me. Feel sorry for me! FEEL FUCKING SORRY FOR ME!

RAGE has taken over my body. RAGE and hatred and anger and fury and condemnation and persecution and judgment and pain. Pain. Pain. Pain. Bewilderment. Haunting.

Tears begin sizzling my cheeks. Scalding and burning. Blistering Bewilderment.

And RAGE.

"GET OUT! GET OUT OF MY HOUSE RIGHT NOW!"

He looks at me. Surprised. Shocked. Dumbfounded. Hurt. Persecuted. Judged.

Understanding.

My heart is bursting, beating, thumping, thudding, trying to find a way out of my body. Trying to find a way out. It needs to run. It needs to hide. It needs to find a way that this is not happening. It needs to find a way that this is not true.

It needs to find a place—a world—where something makes sense. Inside of my body is not this place.

"GET OUT, DAMN IT!"

I sob and scream and RAGE and wail, "GET OUT! GET OUT THIS INSTANT! I NEVER WANT TO SEE YOU AGAIN!"

He walks out the door.

TWENTY-NINE YEARS OLD

(Day Three, 11:11 a.m.)

My life is over. How could this happen? My worst fear is real! He's been desiring other women! He has been cheating on me with images of other fucking women! I'm so stupid! How did I not see this happening! How did I not know?!?!? I'm such an idiot! How did I miss this?!?!?

My life is over. My life is over. My life is over.

I stand in my living room and stare at the window in front of me. In the reflection I see this woman staring back at me. I see this woman that I don't recognize. I see this stranger. This shattered, lost, confused, broken woman. She is heaving for breath. She is shaking uncontrollably. Her face is contorted in a pain so unquestionable, so absolute, so unfathomable, so crushing, so grave, I don't recognize her.

She says, My life is over.

I look back at her. I look at a face that I don't recognize. It is scarred by an anguish and sorrow that is foreign to me. An agony and chaos that even I've never seen. It is the face of agony, chaos, anguish, and sorrow: the face of a dead woman.

I say to the woman, "Yes."

I say, "Yes, your life *is* over."

Your life is over.

Your life is over.

TWENTY-NINE YEARS OLD
(Day 243, 3:33 p.m.)

As I zone into the screen and watch the cursor flash I think over the past five months. The past five years. Hell, the past twenty-nine years. I think about the FLASHES and the WHACKS. I think about the RAGE and the anguish. And, I think about the SMACKS.

The first smack. The tenth smack. The twentieth smack. Mostly though, I think about the last smack. That fateful blow that ultimately took *her* life.

The smack that not only blindsided and bewildered the woman that I was, but also forced her to question everything she had once trusted as true. The smack that forced her to face *all* that she wasn't seeing. That smack that forced her to accept a foreign reality, lay down her sword, emerge from the imaginary safety of her fortress, and succumb to her mortal wounds.

But, through her fall, *I've* been given a gift:

My life is just beginning.

What pack I choose to scamper with and what landscape I may roam, I do not yet know.
However, something enchanting has begun to softly stir within me, inspiring me to listen.
And as I listen I'm beginning to value being thrown to the wolves.

For, I'm beginning to hear the whispers of a calling . . .